THE DAILY HENRY JAMES

THE DAILY

HENRY JAMES

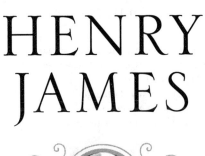

A YEAR OF

QUOTES

FROM THE WORK OF
THE MASTER

FOREWORD BY MICHAEL GORRA

The University of Chicago Press ✳ *Chicago and London*

To My Mother

The University of Chicago Press, Chicago 60637
The University of Chicago Press, Ltd., London
Foreword by Michael Gorra
© 2016 by The University of Chicago
All rights reserved. Published 2016.
Printed in the United States of America

25 24 23 22 21 20 19 18 17 16   1 2 3 4 5

ISBN-13: 978-0-226-40854-5   (paper)
ISBN-13: 978-0-226-40868-2   (e-book)
DOI: 10.7208/chicago/9780226408682.001.0001

This text is based on the original published in 1911; only obvious typographical errors and omissions have been corrected.

I acknowledge, with many thanks, the courtesy of Messrs.
Charles Scribner's Sons, Messrs. Harper & Brothers, The
Houghton Mifflin Company, The Macmillan Company and
Duffield & Company in giving me their permission for the use
of quotations from the writings of Mr. Henry James published
by them and of which they have the copyright.

Evelyn Garnaut Smalley

Library of Congress Control Number: 2016008496

Foreword

This little charmer first appeared as *The Henry James Yearbook* in 1911, bound in a deep burgundy cloth and with a typeface that matched that of the great New York Edition of James's works, an edition that had finished its run only two years before. It offers a quotation for each day of the year, many of them apposite to the season though none of them obvious, and taken from the full range of James's production, the criticism and travel writing as well as the novels and tales.

The book was put out by the Gorham Press, a Boston publisher that, as a Harvard website delicately puts it, produced its things "at their authors' expense." We'd probably call it a vanity press, but in James's day such books were usually described as having been privately printed, a category that included not only the work of his own father but even such classics as *The Education of Henry Adams*. Not that the *Henry James Yearbook* stayed private. H. L. Mencken noticed it in *The Smart Set*, reviewing it alongside Joseph Conrad's *Under Western Eyes*, and in 1912 the English firm of J. M. Dent brought out a trade edition, using sheets imported from Boston.

And then the book more or less vanished. A few older works of criticism list it in their bibliographies, and a small press in Pennsylvania reissued it in 1970. But no scholar has ever paid it much attention, and for decades it survived in the only way that forgotten books do survive: undisturbed in the stacks. Or at least a few of them did, a very few. Today the world's libraries contain scarcely more than a hundred copies, all told, and it might seem little more than a collector's item, a curiosity. Yet there are a number of reasons to look closely at this pocket-sized volume, and aside from the enduring power—the wit, the beauty, the play—of James's own prose, the best of them is the identity of its editor.

Evelyn Garnaut Smalley (1869–1938) was born to American parents in London. Her mother, Phoebe Smalley, was the adopted daughter of the abolitionist Wendell Phillips. Her father, George W. Smalley, had spent his twenties practicing law in Boston, but at the start of the Civil War he took a post on Horace Greeley's *New York Daily Tribune* and in 1862 made his reputation with a battlefield report from Antietam. Afterward he became the paper's London correspondent, and in the 1870s the newly expatriated Henry James was a regular guest at the family's table. Smalley was ten years the novelist's senior; he helped him find a club and a publisher, and James was always grateful. At their house he first met Robert Browning, and learned more about the inside of British politics than he probably cared to. The Smalleys knew everybody, and James joked in a letter to his brother William that they were so worldly as to "dine out three times a day."

Their daughter doesn't figure in James's early letters, but at the turn of the century he told William Dean Howells that he was "very fond" of her, and in old age he wrote to Howells again of his concern over what seemed a difficult life. Evelyn Smalley never married and in middle age still lived with her parents; around 1909 she had some form of breakdown and was for a time institutionalized. "It has been communicated to me," James wrote, "that her infinitely tragic case is one for which no recovery can be hoped." Still, he had heard that her ongoing work on the *Yearbook* seemed therapeutic and wrote that he was eager 'to do what I can'"; the brief prefaces that both he and Howells wrote for this volume should be seen in that light.

But she did recover. I've found two photographs of her, and the first of them, from 1915, shows her on an ocean liner, standing next to her friend, the actress Ellen Terry. The second was taken in 1923 at Les Invalides in Paris. She's wearing a flowing headdress that makes her look like a kind of lay nun and receiving the Legion of Honor from General Henri Gouraud. Evelyn Smalley arrived in France in 1917 with a group from the YMCA whose mission was to provide small comforts for the troops at the very front of the Allied lines. She was stationed at Bouy, to the southeast of Reims. In July 1918 her "hut" came under heavy bombardment, but she refused an order to evacuate and remained at her post until the end of the war; sources in both French and English describe her as appearing in the smoke of battle with a jug of cocoa for any soldier who needed something warm. She also received the Croix de Guerre and died in Pau in 1938.

Smalley's life was in a way very Jamesian, and the book she made pays homage to the figure she had known for the whole of that life. This volume stands as a material witness both to the reading practices of her era and to James's presence in his time. Most of us have a few bits of poetry in our heads, but almost nobody now keeps a commonplace book, a personal anthology of the lines and sentences and paragraphs that have meant the most to us. In earlier ages, however, devoted readers often produced such albums, most of them handwritten and strictly private, though a few did find the fierce legibility of type. This one is a special case since its excerpts all come from the same writer, but it has a precedent in Alexander Main's *Wise, Witty, and Tender Sayings of George Eliot*, first published in 1872. Main's volume sold steadily until the end of the century, and Evelyn Smalley might have thought that this book would have a similar success. But James was never as popular as George Eliot, and in 1911 his fortunes were at their commercial nadir.

Still, his name did stand as a cultural marker, one that even here connotes a fine-grained sense of taste and distinction. (Another such marker was an apartment building called the Henry James, of around the same date, which stood in New York on ground now owned by Columbia University.) And such literary ephemera are more widespread than one might think. Royal Doulton once made figurines of Dickens's characters; in Germany you can buy something called a "Goethe barometer"; and wall calendars often feature quotations, usually of an "inspirational" nature, from this book or that. Yet the fact that James's own ephemera takes the shape of a bound and paradoxically permanent volume suggests that he speaks to a different audience and that Evelyn Smalley aims to fulfill a different set of expectations.

Her choice of passages has its idiosyncrasies. She quotes rather heavily from James's essays on the American poet James Russell Lowell, an intimate family friend, and she's especially drawn to *The Princess Casamassima*, James's fullest account of London life. Yet those excerpts make me want to reread that novel, and indeed the passages she chooses often work to bring a whole book before me, to remind me in a sentence of its essential situation. They are so evocative, in fact, that I've tried in reading month by month to defamiliarize them instead, to forget what I already know and to read these little pieces of prose as though they were indeed freestanding.

That effort has made two things clear. One is James's epigrammatic force. The other, which can be easy to miss when caught by the flow of a narrative, is the extraordinary precision of his descriptive prose, his sheer ability to make you see. I have loved revisiting these passages and hope that in reading them you will find some of the same pleasure.

With thanks to Anne Houston, Barbara Blumenthal, and Karen Kukil of the Smith College Libraries; Levi Stahl and Margaret Hivnor of the University of Chicago Press; and Michael Anesko.

Michael Gorra

NOVEMBER 2015, NORTHAMPTON, MA

Preface

I hope it will be apparent that my work on this book has been a happiness to me. I have also been happy in the thought that it may bring pleasure to some of the many who share in the privilege of companionship with Mr. Henry James's books, and who will understand that the task has been not so much what to select, as what to regretfully omit, and it has been my hope that it may lead some who have missed the precious opportunity of growing up with the books to turn to them. I should then feel I had done the little I actively could in acknowledgement of a life-long obligation; a debt which I am glad to think is constantly increasing. I cannot adequately express my gratitude to Mr. Henry James for the generous sympathy and the appreciation (given to me by him) of my share in the book, and for the gracious kindness that has done so much toward the furtherance of the accomplishment of my purpose. I can only feel both proud and humble and give him once more my deepest thanks.

Evelyn Garnaut Smalley

Introduction

I

THE AUTHOR TO THE PUBLIC

The Athenaeum,
Pall Mall, S. W.
London, June 16, 1910.

I greatly desire to express to all who shall be interested my earnest approval of Miss Evelyn Smalley's *Henry James Year Book*, of which I have seen considerable portions and which she has put together with my full assent and sympathy. To the use she has made of passages from my writings, I greatly and unreservedly subscribe and shall be very happy and must congratulate myself if the present attestation of this fortunately contributes to the publication of the book, and thus to the recognition and reward of so much friendly and discriminating and in every way gracious labour. I take the thing for a very charming and illuminating tribute to the literary performance of

Henry James

ONE OF THE PUBLIC TO THE AUTHOR

My Dear James:

You could hardly have expected a response to your approval for this happily imagined selection before the appeal had reached any of your public in print; but I, who have been privileged to see it in manuscript together with the proofs of the book, make bold to forecast the general satisfaction which I know awaits it.

After being so many years ago your eager editor, and ever since your applausive critic, I ought not to feel bound to insist now upon my delight in the charms of your manner, the depth of your thought, the beauty of your art, which the grouping of these passages freshly witnesses even to such a veteran lover of your work as I; and in fact I do not feel so bound. I do not so much fulfill a duty as indulge a pleasure in owning my surprise at the constant succession of your felicities here. In the relief which their detachment from the context gives them, they have not merely novelty; they seem to have added to their intrinsic value. I have kept asking myself, How came he to think of this or that? How came he to say it in such form that the words as well as the phrases appear of his invention? The delicate wit, the urbane humor, the quiet wisdom, the unfailing good temper—I am sure that the readers who have already affirmed their taste by liking these in your novels and essays will like them the more in an ordering which would be fatal to inferior performance.

That this volume should send people to your books who do not yet know them, as it will surely send people back to them who have long known them, is something greatly to be wished in the interest of literature, and especially of American literature. We do not so abound in masterpieces that we can afford to ignore or neglect the finest of the few we have.

Yours ever,
W. D. Howell

THE DAILY HENRY JAMES

JANUARY

The air, in its windless chill, seemed to tinkle like a crystal, the faintest gradations of tone were perceptible in the sky, the west became deep and delicate, everything grew doubly distinct before taking on the dimness of evening. There were pink flushes on snow, 'tender' reflections on patches of stiffened marsh, sounds of car-bells, no longer vulgar, but almost silvery, on the long bridge, lonely outlines of distant dusky undulations against the fading glow. These agreeable effects used to light up that end of the drawing-room, and Olive often sat at the window with her companion before it was time for the lamp. They admired the sunsets, they rejoiced in the ruddy spots projected upon the parlor-wall, they followed the darkening perspective in fanciful excursions. They watched the stellar points come out at last in a colder heaven, and then, shuddering a little, arm in arm, they turned away with a sense that the winter night was even more cruel than the tyranny of men—turned back to drawn curtains and a brighter fire and a glittering tea-tray and more and more talk.

The Bostonians, 1886

⁓⊙⊙⁓

His sadness has its element of error, but it has also its larger element of wisdom. Life *is*, in fact, a battle. On this point optimists and pessimists agree. Evil is insolent and strong; beauty enchanting but rare; goodness very apt to be weak; folly very apt to be defiant; wickedness to carry the day; imbeciles to be in great places, people of sense in small, and mankind generally unhappy. But the world as it stands is no illusion, no phantasm, no evil dream of a night; we wake up to it again forever and ever; we can neither forget it nor deny it nor dispense with it. We can welcome experience as it comes, and give it what it demands, in exchange for something which is idle to pause to call much or little so long as it contributes to swell the volume of consciousness. In this there is mingled pain and delight, but over the mysterious mixture there hovers a visible rule, that bids us learn to will and seek to understand.

JANUARY 2

THE NEXT TIME, 1895

When he went abroad to gather garlic he came home with heliotrope.

JANUARY 3

"You Americans are almost incredibly romantic."

"Of course we are. That's just what makes everything so nice for us."

"Everything?"

"Well, everything that's nice at all—the world, the beautiful world, or everything in it that is beautiful. I mean we see so much."

JANUARY 4

"Judge everyone and everything for yourself."

"That's what I try to do," said Isabel, "but when you do that people call you conceited."

"You're not to mind them—that's precisely my argument; not to mind what they say about yourself any more than what they say about your friend or your enemy."

—"I think you're right; but there are some things I can't help minding; for instance, when my friend is attacked, or when I myself am praised."

JANUARY 5

THE MARRIAGES, 1892

She was as undomestic as a shop-front and as out of tune as a parrot.

JANUARY 6

THE WINGS OF THE DOVE, 1903

I've often thought success comes to her by the spirit in her that dares and defies her idea not to prove the right one. One has seen it so again and again, in the face of everything, *become* the right one.

JANUARY 7

THE BUNDLE OF LETTERS, 1879

I do love their way of speaking, and sometimes I feel almost as if it would be right to give up trying to learn French, and just try to learn to speak our own tongue as these English speak it. It isn't the things they say so much, though these are often rather curious; but it is in the way they pronounce, and in the sweetness of their voice. It seems as if they must *try* a good deal to talk like that; but these English that are here don't seem to try at all, either to speak or do anything else.

JANUARY 8

The English writer wants to make sure, first of all, of your moral judgment; the French is willing, while it waits a little, to risk, for the sake of his subject and your interest, your spiritual salvation.

JANUARY 9

"You must take us as we come—with all our imperfections on our heads. Of course we haven't your country life, and your old ruins, and your great estates, and your leisure-class and all that. But if we haven't, I should think you might find it a pleasant change—I think any country is pleasant where they have pleasant manners."

JANUARY 10

"We must do our duty—when once we see it. I didn't know—I didn't understand. But now I do. It's when one's eyes are opened that the wrong is wrong."

JANUARY 11

THE ART OF FICTION, 1884

But the only condition that I can think of attaching to the composition of the novel is, as I have already said, that it be sincere. This freedom is a splendid privilege, and the first lesson of the young novelist is to learn to be worthy of it.

JANUARY 12

THE ASPERN PAPERS, 1888

It is not supposed to be the nature of women to rise as a general thing to the largest and most liberal view—I mean of a practical scheme; but it has struck me that they sometimes throw off a bold conception—such as a man wouldn't have risen to—with singular serenity.

JANUARY 13

THE REVERBERATOR, 1888

"Against Americans I have nothing to say; some of them are the best thing the world contains. That's precisely why one can choose."

JANUARY 14

She was always black-robed, as if she had had a succession of sorrows. People were not poor, after all, whom so many losses would overtake; they were positively rich when they had so much to give up.

JANUARY 15

"One was no doubt a meddlesome fool; one always *is*, to think one sees peoples' lives for them better than they see them for themselves. I always pay for it sooner or later, my sociable, my damnable, my unnecessary interest."

JANUARY 16

"My dear young lady," said Mrs. Touchett, "there are as many points of view in the world as there are people of sense. You may say that doesn't make them very numerous! American? Never in the world; that's shockingly narrow. My point of view, thank God, is personal!"

"She does care for him you know," said Mr. Langdon.

—Mitchy, at this, gave a long, wide, glare.

"With Nanda," he next added, "it's deep."

His companion took it from him. "Deep."

"And yet somehow it isn't abject."

The old man wondered. "'Abject'?"

"I mean it isn't pitiful. In its way," Mitchy developed, "it's happy."

This, too, though rather ruefully, Mr. Langdon would take from him. "Yes—in its way."

"Any passion so great, so complete," Mitchy went on, is—satisfied or unsatisfied—a life."

Apologies, Mrs. Touchett intimated, were of no more use than soap-bubbles, and she herself never dealt in such articles. One either did the thing or one didn't, and what one would quite differently have done belonged to the sphere of the irrelevant, like the idea of a future life or of the origin of things.

JANUARY 19

"She's like a revolving lighthouse; pitch darkness alternating with a dazzling brilliancy."

JANUARY 20

In that lively sense of the immediate which is the very air of a child's mind, the past, on each occasion, became for her as indistinct as the future: she surrendered herself to the actual with a good faith that might have been touching to either parent.

JANUARY 21

"Haven't you discovered that the American girl expects something especially adapted to herself? It's very well in Europe to have a few phrases that will do for any girl. The American girl isn't any girl; she's a remarkable individual in a remarkable genus."

JANUARY 22

She was only a suburban young woman in a sailor hat, and he a young man destitute in strictness of occasion for a "topper"; but they felt that they had in a peculiar way the freedom of the town, and the town, if it did nothing else, gave a range to the spirit.

JANUARY 23

People may like George Sand or not, but they can hardly deny that she is the great *improvisatrice* of literature—the writer who best answers to Shelley's description of the sky-lark singing "in profuse strains of unpremeditated art." No writer has produced such great effects with an equal absence of premeditation.

JANUARY 24

There was something a failure was, a failure in the market, that a success somehow wasn't. A success was as prosaic as a good dinner: there was nothing more to be said about it than that you had had it; and who but vulgar people, in such a case, made gloating remarks about the courses?

JANUARY 25

EUGENE PICKERING, 1874

"The pearl of wisdom," I cried, "is love; honest love in the most convenient concentration of experience! I advise you to fall in love."

JANUARY 26

THE WINGS OF THE DOVE, 1903

Compressed and concentrated, confined to a single sharp pang or two, but none the less in wait for him there and lifting its head as that of a snake in the garden, was the disconcerting sense that "respect," in their game, seemed somehow—he scarce knew what to call it—a fifth wheel to the coach. It was properly an inside thing, not an outside, a thing to make love greater, not to make happiness less.

JANUARY 27

DAISY MILLER, 1878

It seemed to him also that Daisy had never looked so pretty; but this had been an observation of his whenever he met her.

JANUARY 28

THE REVERBERATOR, 1888

Like many unoccupied young men at the present hour he gave much attention to art, lived as much as possible in that alternative world, where leisure and vagueness are so mercifully relieved of their crudity.

JANUARY 29

THE PRINCESS CASAMASSIMA, 1886

She appeared very nearly as resigned to the troubles of others as she was to her own.

JANUARY 30

She convinced him, rather effectually, that even in a great democracy there are human differences, and that American life was full of social distinctions, of delicate shades, which foreigners are often too stupid to perceive.

JANUARY 31

It was one of the quiet instants that sometimes settle more matters than the outbreaks dear to the historic muse.

FEBRUARY

The winter was not over, but the spring had begun, and the smoky London air allowed the baffled citizens, by way of a change, to see through it. The town could refresh its recollections of the sky, and the sky could ascertain the geographical position of the town. The essential dimness of the low perspectives had by no means disappeared, but it had loosened its folds; it lingered as a blur of mist, interwoven with pretty suntints and faint transparencies. There was warmth and there was light, and a view of the shutters of shops, and the church bells were ringing.

The Princess Casamassima, 1886

FEBRUARY 1

THE MADONNA OF THE FUTURE, 1873

"But meanwhile, the painter's idea had taken wings. No lovely human outline could charm it to vulgar fact. He saw the fair form made perfect; he rose to the vision without tremor, without effort of wing; he communed with it face to face, and resolved into finer and lovelier truth the purity which completes it as the fragrance completes the rose. That's what they call idealism; the word's vastly abused, but the thing's good. It's my own creed at any rate."

FEBRUARY 2

THE WINGS OF THE DOVE, 1903

She had arts and idiosyncrasies of which no great account could have been given, but which were a daily grace if you lived with them; such as the art of being almost tragically impatient and yet making it as light as air; of being inexplicably sad and yet making it as clear as noon; of being unmistakably gay, and yet making it as soft as dusk.

FEBRUARY 3

She ultimately made up her mind that to be rich was a virtue, because it was to be able to *do*, and to do was sweet. It was the contrary of weakness. To be weak was, for a young lady, rather graceful, but, after all, as Isabel said to herself, there was a larger grace than that.

FEBRUARY 4

His idea of loyalty was that he should scarcely smoke a cigar unless his friend were there to take another, and he felt rather mean if he went round alone to get shaved.

FEBRUARY 5

The recurrence of opportunity to observe them together would have taught a spectator that—on Mrs. Brook's side, doubtless, more particularly—their relation was governed by two or three remarkably established and, as might have been said, refined laws, the spirit of which was to guard against the vulgarity so often coming to the surface between parent and child. That they *were* as good friends as if Nanda had not been her daughter was a truth that no passage between them might fail in one way or another to illustrate.

FEBRUARY 6

RODERICK HUDSON, 1875

"The whole matter of genius is a mystery. It bloweth where it listeth and we know nothing of its mechanism. If it gets out of order we can't mend it; if it breaks down altogether we can't set it going again. We must let it choose its own pace and hold our breath lest it should lose its balance. It's dealt out in different doses, in big cups and little, and when you have consumed your portion it's as *naif* to ask for more as it was for Oliver Twist to ask for more porridge. Lucky for you if you've got one of the big cups; we drink them down in the dark, and we can't tell their size until we tip them up and hear the last gurgle. Those of some men last for life; those of others for a couple of years."

FEBRUARY 7

This was all he had to point to. However he pointed to nothing; which was very possibly just a sign of his real cleverness, one of those that the really clever had in common with the really void.

FEBRUARY 8

THE PRINCESS CASAMASSIMA, 1886

Strange enough it was, and a proof, surely, of our little hero's being a genuine artist, that the impressions he had accumulated during the last few months appeared to mingle and confound themselves with the very sources of his craft and to be susceptible of technical representation.

FEBRUARY 9

GEORGE SAND, 1878

George Sand's optimism, her idealism, are very beautiful, and the source of that impression of largeness, luminosity and liberality which she makes upon us, but we suspect that something even better in a novelist is that tender appreciation of actuality which makes even the application of a single coat of rose-color an act of violence.

FEBRUARY 10

THE AMBASSADORS, 1903

"Well," said little Bilham, "you're not a person to whom it's easy to tell things you don't want to know. Though it *is* easy, I admit—it's quite beautiful," he benevolently added, "when you do want to."

FEBRUARY 11

THE ALTAR OF THE DEAD, 1895

He thought, for a long time, of how the closed eyes of dead women could still live—how they could open again, in a quiet lamplit room, long after they had looked their last. They had looks that remained, as great poets had quoted lines.

FEBRUARY 12

This love of life was so strong in him that he could lose himself in little diversions as well as in big books. He was fond of everything human and natural, everything that had color and character, and no gayety, no sense of comedy, was ever more easily kindled by contact. When he was not surrounded by great pleasures he could find his account in small ones, and no situation could be dull for a man in whom all reflection, all reaction, was witty.

FEBRUARY 13

THE PORTRAIT OF A LADY, 1881

"It's a sign that I am growing old—that I like to talk with younger people. I think it's a very pretty compensation. If we can't have youth within us we can have it outside of us, and I really think we see it and feel it better that way. Of course we must be in sympathy with it—that I shall always be. I don't know that I shall ever be ill-natured with old people. I hope not; there are certainly some old people that I adore. But I shall never be ill-natured with the young; they touch me too much."

FEBRUARY 14

THE MARRIAGES, 1892

Mrs. Churchley had every intention of getting, as she would have said—she was perpetually using the expression—into touch; but her good intentions were as depressing as a tailor's misfits.

FEBRUARY 15

THE LIAR, 1889

When he was working well he found himself in that happy state—the happiest of all for an artist—in which things in general contribute to the particular idea and fall in with it, help it on and justify it, so that he feels for the hour as if nothing in the world can happen to him, even if it come in the guise of disaster or suffering, that will not be an enhancement of his subject.

FEBRUARY 16

THE PRINCESS CASAMASSIMA, 1886

"Our troubles don't kill us, Prince; it's we who must try to kill them. I have buried not a few."

FEBRUARY 17

With his genius in his eyes, his manners on his lips, his long career behind him and his honors and rewards all round, the great artist, in the course of a single sustained look and a few words of delight at receiving him, affected our friend as a dazzling prodigy of type.

FEBRUARY 18
THE GOLDEN BOWL, 1904

She had lived long enough to make out for herself that any deep-seated passion has its pangs as well as its joys, and that we are made by its aches and its anxieties most richly conscious of it.

FEBRUARY 19
THE PENSION BEAUREPAS, 1880

It sounds as if life went on in a very makeshift fashion at the Pension Beaurepas—as if the tone of the establishment was sordid. But such was not at all the case. We were simply very bourgeois; we prac-

tised the good old Genevese principle of not sacrific-
ing to appearances. This is an excellent principle—
when you have the reality.

FEBRUARY 20
THE MADONNA OF THE FUTURE, 1873

"The mystery was suddenly solved: my friend was
an American! He must have been to take the pictur-
esque so prodigiously to heart!"

FEBRUARY 21
THE WINGS OF THE DOVE, 1903

The single thing that was clear, in complications,
was that, whatever happened, one was to behave
as a gentleman—to which was added indeed the
perhaps slightly less shining truth that complications might sometimes have their tedium beguiled
by a study of the question how a gentleman would
behave.

FEBRUARY 22

JAMES RUSSELL LOWELL, 1891

His America was a country worth hearing about, a magnificent conception, an admirably consistent and lovable object of allegiance. If the sign that in Europe one knew him best by was his intense national consciousness, one felt that this consciousness could not sit lightly on a man in whom it was the strongest form of piety. Fortunately for him and for his friends he was one of the most whimsical, one of the wittiest of human beings, so that he could play with his patriotism and make it various. All the same, one felt in it, in talk, the depth of passion that hums through his finest verse—almost the only passion that, to my sense, his poetry contains—the accent of chivalry, of the lover, the knight ready to do battle for his mistress.

[JAMES RUSSELL LOWELL BORN ON THIS DAY IN 1819]

FEBRUARY 23

A LANDSCAPE PAINTER, 1866

"It *is* your own fault if people don't care for you; you don't care for them. That you should be indifferent to their good opinion is all very well; but you don't care for their indifference."

FEBRUARY 24

It came back—to his own previous perception—that of the Prince's inability, in any matter in which he was concerned, to *conclude*. The idiosyncrasy, for him, at each stage, had to be demonstrated. And how, when you came to that, *could* you know that a horse wouldn't shy at a brass-band, in a country road, because it didn't shy at a traction engine? It might have been brought up to traction engines without having been brought up to brass-bands.

FEBRUARY 25

"Try and make a clever woman of her, Lavinia; I should like her to be a clever woman."

"My dear Austin, do you think it is better to be clever than to be good?"

"Good for what?"—asked the doctor. "You are good for nothing unless you are clever."

FEBRUARY 26

At the back of his head, behind everything, was the sense that she was—there, before him, close to him, in vivid, imperative form—one of the rare women he had so often heard of, read of, thought of, but never met, whose very presence, look, voice, the mere contemporaneous fact of whom, from the moment it was at all presented, made a relation of mere recognition.

FEBRUARY 27

"You're so wonderful to your friends"—oh, she could let him see that she knew!—"and in such different and exquisite ways. There are those—who get everything out of you and whom you really appear to like, or at least to put up with, just *for* that. Then there are those who ask nothing—and whom you like in spite of it."

FEBRUARY 28

When Milly smiled it was a public event—when she didn't it was a chapter of history.

FEBRUARY 29

Her splendid hair seemed to shine; her cheek and chin had a curve which struck him by its fineness; her eyes and lips were full of smiles and greetings. She had appeared to him before as a creature of brightness, but how she lighted up the place, she irradiated, she made everything that surrounded her of no consequence; dropping upon the shabby sofa with an effect as charming as if she had been a nymph sinking on a leopard-skin, and with the native sweetness of her voice forcing him to listen till she spoke again.

MARCH

The hour I first recall was a morning of winter drizzle and mist, of dense fog in the Bay, one of the strangest sights of which I was on my way to enjoy; and I had stopped in the heart of the business quarter to pick up a friend who was to be my companion. The weather, such as it was, worked wonders for the upper reaches of the buildings, round which it drifted and hung very much as about the flanks and summits of emergent mountain-masses—for, to be just all round, there *was* some evidence of their having a message for the eyes. Let me parenthesize, once for all, that there are other glimpses of this message, up and down the city, frequently to be caught; lights and shades of winter and summer air, of the literally "finishing" afternoon in particular, when refinement of modelling descends from the skies and lends the white towers, all new and crude and commercial and over-windowed as they are, a fleeting distinction.

The American Scene, 1907

⁓⊙⊙⁓

MARCH 1

He had turned his steps, for the pleasure of memory, to Fresh Pond, dear to the muses of youth, the Sunday afternoons of spring, and had to accept there his clearest vision perhaps of the new differences and indifferences. The desecrated, the destroyed resort had favored, save on rare feast days, the single stroll, or at the worst the double, dedicated to shared literary secrets; which was why I almost angrily missed, among the ruins, what I had mainly gone back to recover—some echo of the dreams of youth, the titles of tales, the communities of friendship, the sympathies and patience, in fine, of dear W. D. H.

MARCH 2

"How you must have loved him!"
"Women are not like men. They can love even where they've suffered."

"I should be interested to see some sense you don't possess."

"The moral, dear Mrs. Assingham. I mean, always, as you others consider it. I've of course something that in our poor dear backward old Rome sufficiently passes for it. But it's no more like yours than the tortuous stone staircase—half ruined into the bargain!—in some castle of our *quattro cento* is like the lightning elevator in one of Mr. Verver's fifteen-story buildings. Your moral sense works by steam—it sends you up like a rocket. Ours is slow and steep and unlighted, with so many of the steps missing that—well, that it's as short, in almost any case, to turn round and come down again."

MARCH 4

POOR RICHARD, 1867

He had told her that she was an enchantress, and this assertion, too, had its measure of truth. But her spell was a steady one; it sprang not from her beauty, her wit, her grace—it sprang from her character. In other words Gertrude exercised the magnificent power of making her lover forget her face.

MARCH 5

Densher himself was not unconscious in respect to this of a certain broad brotherhood with Mrs. Stringham; wondering indeed, while he followed the talk, how it might move American nerves. He had only heard of them before, but in his recent tour he had caught them in the fact, and there was now a moment or two when it came to him that he had perhaps—and not in the way of an escape—taken a lesson from them.

MARCH 6

Du Maurier possesses in perfection the independence of the genuine artist in the presence of a hundred worldly superstitions and absurdities. We have said, however, that the morality, so to speak, of his drawings was a subordinate question: what we wished to insist upon is their completeness, their grace, their beauty, their rare pictorial character.

"A large fortune means freedom, and I am afraid of that. It's such a fine thing and one should make such a good use of it. If one didn't, one would be ashamed. And one must always be thinking—it's a constant effort. I am not sure it's not a greater happiness to be powerless."

"For weak people I have no doubt it's a greater happiness. For weak people the effort not to be contemptible must be great."

"I fancy it is our peculiar good luck that we don't see the limits of our minds," said Rowland. "We are young, compared with what we may one day be. That belongs to youth; it is perhaps the best part of it. They say that old people do find themselves at last face to face with a solid blank wall and stand thumping against it in vain. It resounds, it seems to have something beyond it, but it won't move! That's only a reason for living with open doors as long as we can."

For these candid minds the newspapers and all they contained were a part of the general fatality of things, of the recurrent freshness of the universe, coming out like the sun in the morning or the stars at night.

MARCH 10

THE GOLDEN BOWL, 1904

"Do you consider that we are careless of mankind?— living as we do in the biggest crowd in the world, and running about always pursued and pursuing."

"Well I don't know. We get nothing but the fun, do we?"

"No," she hastened to declare; "we certainly get nothing but the fun."

"We do it all," he had remarked, "so beautifully."

"We do it all so beautifully. I see what you mean."

"Well, I mean too," he had gone on, "that we haven't, no doubt, enough, the sense of difficulty."

"Enough? Enough for what?"

"Enough not to be selfish."

MARCH 11

In those days in New York there were still a few altar fires flickering in the temple of Republican simplicity, and Dr. Sloper would have been glad to see his daughter present herself, with a classic grace, as priestess of this mild faith.

MARCH 12

THE WINGS OF THE DOVE, 1903

It was rich, romantic, abysmal, to have, as was evident, thousands and thousands a year, to have youth and intelligence and, if not beauty, at least in equal measure, a high, dim, charming, ambiguous oddity, which was even better, and then, on top of all, to enjoy boundless freedom, the freedom of the wind in the desert—it was unspeakably touching to be so equipped and yet to have been reduced by fortune to little humble-minded mistakes.

MARCH 13

THE ALTAR OF THE DEAD, 1895

But the time he gave to his devotion came to seem to him more a contribution to his other interests

than a betrayal of them. Even a loaded life might
be easier when one had added a new necessity to it.

MARCH 14

THE GOLDEN BOWL, 1904

"One mustn't take advantage of her character—one
mustn't, if not for *her*, at least for one's self. She
saves one such trouble."
"She certainly *gives* one no trouble.—She's not self-
ish—God forgive her!—enough."
"That's what I mean—she's not selfish enough.
There's nothing, absolutely, that one *need* do for her.
She's so modest—she doesn't miss things. I mean
if you love her rather, I should say, if she loves you.
She lets it go."

MARCH 15

THE PRINCESS CASAMASSIMA, 1886

He had still a delighted attention to spare for
the green dimness of leafy lanes, the attraction
of meadow-paths that led from stile to stile and
seemed a clue to some pastoral happiness, some
secret of the fields; the hedges thick with flowers,
bewilderingly common, for which he knew no
names, the picture-making quality of thatched cottages, the mystery and sweetness of blue distances,

the bloom of rural complexions, the quaintness of little girls bobbing curtsies by waysides (a sort of homage he had never prefigured); the soft sense of the turf under feet that had never ached but from paving stones.

MARCH 16
THE AWKWARD AGE, 1899

"My dear thing, it all comes back, as everything always does, simply to personal pluck. It's only a question, no matter when or where, of having enough."

MARCH 17
THE EUROPEANS, 1878

It is beside the matter to say he had a good conscience; for the best conscience is a sort of self-reproach, and this young man's brilliantly healthy nature spent itself in objective good intentions which were ignorant of any test save exactness in hitting the mark.

MARCH 18

Once more, as a man conscious of having known many women, he could assist, as he would have called it, at the recurrent, the predestined phenomenon, the thing always as certain as sunrise or the coming round of Saints' days, the doing by the woman of the thing that gave her away. She did it, ever, inevitably, infallibly—she couldn't possibly not do it. It was her nature, it was her life, and the man could always expect it without lifting a finger.

MARCH 19

Of course the danger of a high spirit is the danger of inconsistency—the danger of keeping up the flag after the place has surrendered; a sort of behavior so anomalous as to be almost a dishonor to the flag.

MARCH 20

She thought of the lively and chatty letters that they had always seen in the papers and wondered whether they *all* meant a violation of sanctities, a convulsion of homes, a burning of smitten faces, a rupture of girls' engagements.

MARCH 21

THE GOLDEN BOWL, 1904

An ability, of a truth, is an aid to success; it has even been known to be the principle of large accumulations.

MARCH 22

EUROPE, 1900

Jane's yearning was the sharpest. She struggled with it as people at Brookbridge mostly struggled with what they liked, but fate, by threatening to prevent what she *dis*liked, and what was therefore duty— which was to stay at home instead of Maria—had bewildered her, I judged, not a little.

MARCH 23

A LANDSCAPE PAINTER, 1866

"There are not five people in the world who really care for me."—"*Really* care? I am afraid you look too close. And then I think five good friends is a very large number. I think myself very well off with half a one. But if you are friendless it's probably your own fault."

MARCH 24
THE BOSTONIANS, 1886

It was recognized, liberally enough, that there were many things—perhaps even too many—New York *could* give; but this was felt to make no difference in the constant fact that what you had most to do under the discipline of life, or of death, was really to feel your situation as grave. Boston could help you to that as nothing else could.

MARCH 25
THE AWKWARD AGE, 1899

Nanda had gathered up, for that matter, early in life, a flower of maternal wisdom: "People talk about the conscience, but it seems to me one must just bring it up to a certain point and leave it there. You can let your conscience alone if you're nice to the second housemaid."

MARCH 26

"To be young and elastic, and yet old enough and wise enough to discriminate and reflect, and to come to Italy for the first time—that's one of the greatest pleasures life has to offer us."

MARCH 27

No one could explain better when needful, nor put more conscience into an account or a report; which burden of conscience is perhaps exactly the reason why his heart always sank when the clouds of explanation gathered. His highest ingenuity was in keeping the sky of life clear of them. Whether or no he had a grand idea of the lucid, he held that nothing ever was in fact—for anyone else—explained. One went through the vain motions, but it was mostly a waste of life. A personal relation was a relation only so long as people perfectly understood it, or better still didn't care if they didn't. From the moment they cared if they didn't it was living by the sweat of one's brow; and the sweat of one's brow was just what one might buy one's self off from by keeping the ground free of the wild weed of delusion. This easily grew too fast.

MARCH 28

"Now the question is whether you can do it for two or
three. Is that the stuff you're made of?"
"I could do it for one, if you were the one."
"The 'one' is of course oneself—one's conscience,
one's idea, the singleness of one's aim. I think of
that pure spirit as a man thinks of a woman whom,
in some detested hour of his youth he has loved and
forsaken. She haunts him with reproachful eyes,
she lives forever before him."

MARCH 29

"It's so charming being liked," she went on, "without
being approved."

MARCH 30

He had been wondering a minute ago if the boy
weren't a pagan, and he found himself wondering
now if he weren't by chance a gentleman. It didn't
in the least, on the spot, spring up helpfully for him
that a person couldn't at the same time be both.
There was nothing at this moment in the air to chal-

lenge the combination; there was everything, on the contrary, to give it something of a flourish.

MARCH 31

WHAT MAISIE KNEW, 1898

And presently she was close to him in one of the chairs, with the prettiest of pictures, the sheen of the lake through other trees before them and the sound of birds, the splash of boats, the play of children in the air.

APRIL

The beauty of the 'Elevated' was that it took you up to the Park and brought you back in a few minutes, and you had all the rest of the hour to walk about and see the place. It was so pleasant now that one was glad to see it twice over. The long, narrow inclosure, across which the houses in the streets that border it look at each other with their glittering windows, bristled with the raw delicacy of April, and, in spite of its rockwork grottoes and tunnels, its pavilions and statues, its too immense paths and pavements, lakes too big for the landscape and bridges too big for the lakes, expressed all the fragrance and freshness of the most charming moment of the year.

The Bostonians, 1886

APRIL 1

"But do you know my own thought? Nothing is so idle as to talk about our want of a nutritive soil, of opportunity, of inspiration, and all the rest of it. The worthy part is to do something fine! There's no law in our glorious Constitution against that. Invent, create, achieve! No matter if you have to study fifty times as much as one of these! What else are you an artist for?"

APRIL 2

Two of these happy summer days on the occasion of his last visit to Whitby are marked possessions of my memory; one of them a ramble on the warm, wide moors, after a rough lunch at a little, stony upland inn, in company charming and intimate, the thought of which to-day is a reference to a double loss. [AN ALLUSION TO THE LATE ALFRED ST. JOHNSTON]

APRIL 3

No portrait that I have seen gives any idea of his expression. There were so many things in it, and they chased each other in and out of his face. I have seen people who were grave and gay in quick alternation; but Mark Ambient was grave and gay at one and the same moment.

APRIL 4

THE EUROPEANS, 1878

His faculty of enjoyment was so large, so unconsciously eager, that one felt it had a permanent advance on embarrassment and sorrow.

APRIL 5

THE AWKWARD AGE, 1899

Mr. Longdon hadn't made his house, he had simply lived it, and the "taste" of the place—Mitchy in certain connections abominated the word—was nothing more than the beauty of his life.

APRIL 6

THE GOLDEN BOWL, 1904

"She lets it go."
"She lets what?"
"Anything—anything that you might do and that

you don't. She lets everything go but her own disposition to be kind to you. It's of herself that she asks efforts—so far as she ever *has* to ask them. She hasn't, much. She does everything herself. And that's terrible."

APRIL 7

WHAT MAISIE KNEW, 1898

The joy of the world so waylaid the steps of his friends that little by little the spirit of hope filled the air and finally took possession of the scene.

APRIL 8

THE LESSON OF THE MASTER, 1892

"She gives away because she overflows. She has her own feelings, her own standards; she doesn't keep remembering that she must be proud."

APRIL 9

THE AMBASSADORS, 1903

He had not had the gift of making the most of what he tried, and if he had tried and tried again—none but himself knew how often—it appeared to have been that he might demonstrate what else, in default of that, *could* be made. Old ghosts of experiments came back to him, old drudgeries and delusions and disgusts, old recoveries with their relapses, old fevers with their chills, broken moments of good faith, others of still better doubt; adventures, for the most part, of the sort qualified as lessons.

APRIL 10

THE PRINCESS CASAMASSIMA, 1886

There were things in his heart and a torment and a hidden passion in his life which he should be glad enough to lay open to some woman. He believed that perhaps this would be the cure ultimately; that in return for something he might drop, syllable by syllable, into a listening feminine ear, certain other words would be spoken to him which would make his pain forever less sharp.

APRIL 11

THE WINGS OF THE DOVE, 1903

She was somehow at this hour a very happy woman, and a part of her happiness might precisely have been that her affections and her views were moving as never before in concert.

APRIL 12
THE AUTHOR OF BELTRAFFIO, 1885

It was the point of view of the artist to whom every manifestation of human energy was a thrilling spectacle, and who felt it forever the desire to resolve his experience of life into a literary form.

APRIL 13
WASHINGTON SQUARE, 1881

Washington Square, where the doctor built himself a handsome, modern, wide-fronted house, with a big balcony before the drawing-room windows, and a flight of white marble steps ascending to a portal which was also faced with white marble. This structure, and many of its neighbors, which it exactly resembled, were supposed, forty years ago, to embody the last results of architectural science, and they remain to this day very solid and honorable dwellings.

APRIL 14

"Fancy an artist with a plurality of standards to *do* it: to do it and make it divine is the only thing he has to think about. 'Is it done or not?' is his only question."

APRIL 15

The ideal of quiet and of genteel retirement, in 1835, was found in Washington Square. In front was the large quadrangle, containing a considerable quantity of inexpensive vegetation, enclosed by a wooden paling, which increased its rural and accessible appearance; and round the corner was the more august precinct of the Fifth Avenue, taking its origin at this point with a spacious and confident air which already marked it for high destinies. I know not whether it be owing to the tenderness of early associations, but this portion of New York appears to many persons the most engaging. It has a kind of established repose which is not of frequent occurrence in other quarters of the long shrill city; it has a riper, richer, more honourable look than any of the upper ramifications of the great longitudinal thoroughfare—the look of having had something of a social history. It was here, as you might have been informed on good authority, that you had come into a world which appeared to offer a variety of sources of interest; it was here that your grandmother lived, in venerable solitude, and dispensed a hospitality which commended itself alike to the infant imagination and the infant palate; it was here that you took your first walks abroad, following the nursery-maid with unequal step and sniffing up the strange odour of the ailanthus-trees which at that time formed the principal umbrage of the square, and diffused an aroma that you were not yet critical enough to dislike as it deserved; it was here, finally, that your first school, kept by a broad-bosomed, broad-based old lady with a ferule, who was always having tea in a blue cup, with a saucer that didn't match, enlarged the circle both of your observations and your sensations.

APRIL 16

THE FIGURE IN THE CARPET, 1896

"By my little point I mean—what shall I call it?— the particular thing I've written my books most *for*. Isn't there for every writer a particular thing of that sort, the thing that most makes him apply himself, the thing without the effort to achieve which he wouldn't write at all, the very passion of his passion, the part of the business in which, for him, the flame of art burns most intensely? Well, it's *that*!"

APRIL 17

Beyond the lawn the house was before him, old, square, red-roofed, well assured of its right to the place it took up in the world. This was a considerable space—in the little world at least of Beccles—and the look of possession had everything mixed with it, in the form of old windows and doors, the tone of old red surfaces, the style of old white facings, the age of old high creepers, the long confirmation of time. Suggestive of panelled rooms, of precious mahogany, of portraits of women dead, of colored china glimmering through glass doors, and delicate silver reflected on bared tables, the thing was one of those impressions of a particular period that it takes two centuries to produce.

APRIL 18

"The other day when I was looking at Michael Angelo's Moses I was seized with a kind of defiance—a reaction against all this mere passive enjoyment of grandeur. It was a rousing great success, certainly, that sat there before me, but somehow it wasn't an inscrutable mystery, and it seemed to me, not perhaps that I should some day do as well, but that at least I *might*!"

"As you say, you can but try," said Rowland. "Success is only passionate effort."

APRIL 19

THE ART OF FICTION, 1884

There is one point at which the moral sense and the artistic sense lie very near together, that is in the light of the very obvious truth that the deepest quality of a work of art will always be the quality of the mind of the producer. In proportion as that intelligence is fine will the novel, the picture, the statue partake of the substance of beauty and truth. To be constituted of such elements is, to my vision, to have purpose enough.

APRIL 20

THE NEXT TIME, 1895

Popular?—how on earth could it be popular? The thing was charming with all his charm and powerful with all his power; it was an unscrupulous, an unsparing, a shameless, merciless masterpiece.

APRIL 21

She was barely conscious of the loveliness of the day, the perfect weather, all suffused and tinted with spring which sometimes descends upon New York when the winds of March have been stilled. She held her way to the Square, which, as all the world knows, is of great extent and open to the encircling street. The trees and grass-plats had begun to bud and sprout, the fountains plashed in the sunshine, the children of the quarter, both the dingier types from the south side, who played games that required much chalking of the paved walks, and much sprawling and crouching there, under the feet of passers, and the little curled and feathered people who drove their hoops under the eyes of French nurse maids—all the infant population filled the vernal air with small sounds which had a crude, tender quality, like the leaves and the thin herbage.

APRIL 22

"I'm sure you've an excellent spirit; but don't try to bear more things than you need." Which after an instant he further explained. "Hard things have come to you in youth, but you mustn't think life will be for you all hard things. You've the right to be happy. You must make up your mind to it. You must accept any form in which happiness may come."

APRIL 23
THE BIRTHPLACE, 1903

He felt as if a window had opened into a great green woodland, a woodland that had a name, glorious, immortal, that was peopled with vivid figures, each of them renowned, and that gave out a murmur, deep as the sound of the sea, which was the rustle in forest shade of all the poetry, the beauty, the colour of life.

"It's rather a pity, you know, that He *isn't* here. I mean as Goethe's at Weimar. For Goethe *is* at Weimar." "Yes, my dear; that's Goethe's bad luck. There he sticks. *This* man [Shakespeare] isn't anywhere. I defy you to catch Him." "Why not say beautifully," the young woman laughed, "that, like the wind, He's everywhere?"

APRIL 24
THE NEXT TIME, 1895

Her disappointments and eventually her privations had been many, her discipline severe; but she had ended by accepting the long grind of life, and was now quite willing to be ground in good company.

APRIL 25
THE GOLDEN BOWL, 1904

Their rightness, the justification of everything—something they so felt the pulse of—sat there with them; but mightn't the moment possibly count for them as the dawn of the discovery that it doesn't always meet *all* contingencies to be right?

APRIL 26
THE TRAGIC MUSE, 1889

The other, though only asking to live without too many questions and work without too many disasters, to be glad and sorry in short on easy terms, had become aware of a certain social tightness, of the fact that life is crowded and passion restless, accident frequent and community inevitable. Everybody with whom one had relations had other relations too, and even optimism was a mixture and peace an embroilment. The only chance was to let everything be embroiled but one's temper and everything spoiled but one's work.

APRIL 27

ANTHONY TROLLOPE, 1883

His great, his inestimable merit was a complete appreciation of the usual. Trollope, therefore, with his eyes comfortably fixed on the familiar, the actual, was far from having invented a new category; his distinction is that in resting just there his vision took in so much of the field. And then he *felt* all daily and immediate things as well as saw them; felt them in a simple, direct, salubrious way, with their sadness, their gladness, their charm, their comicality, all their obvious and measurable meanings.

APRIL 28

THE ALTAR OF THE DEAD, 1895

Stransom sincerely considered that he had forgiven him; how little he had achieved the miracle that she had achieved! His forgiveness was silence, but hers was mere unuttered sound.

APRIL 29

THE BEAST IN THE JUNGLE, 1903

He told her everything, all his secrets. He talked and talked, often making her think of herself as a lean, stiff person, destitute of skill or art, but with ear enough to be performed to, sometimes strangely touched, at moments completely ravished, by a fine violinist. He was her fiddler and genius, she was sure neither of her taste nor of his tunes, but if she could do nothing else for him she could hold the case while he handled the instrument.

APRIL 30

THE PRINCESS CASAMASSIMA, 1886

Such a reflection as that, however, ceased to trouble him after he had passed out of doors and begun to roam through the park, into which he let himself loose at first, and then, in narrowing circles, through the nearer grounds. He rambled for an hour in a state of breathless ecstasy; brushing the dew from the deep fern and bracken and the rich borders of the garden, tasting the fragrant air and stopping everywhere, in murmuring rapture, at the touch of some exquisite impression. His whole walk was peopled with recognitions; he had been dreaming all his life of just such a place and such objects, such a morning and such a chance. It was the last of April and everything was fresh and vivid; the great trees, in the early air, were a blur of tender shoots. Round the admirable house he revolved repeatedly—there was something in the way the gray walls rose from the green lawn that brought tears to his eyes. The spectacle of long duration unassociated with some sordid infirmity or poverty was new to him; he had lived with people among whom old age meant, for the most part, a grudged and degraded survival. In the majestic preservation of Medley there was a kind of serenity of success, an accumulation of dignity and honour.

MAY

He had for the next hour an accidental air of looking for it in the windows of shops; he came down the Rue de la Paix in the sun and, passing across the Tuileries and the river, indulged more than once—as if on finding himself determined—in a sudden pause before the bookstalls of the opposite quay. In the garden of the Tuileries he had lingered, on two or three spots, to look; it was as if the wonderful Paris spring had stayed him as he roamed. The prompt Paris morning struck its cheerful notes—in a soft breeze and a sprinkled smell, in a light flit, over the garden-floor, of bareheaded girls with the buckled strap of oblong boxes, in the type of ancient thrifty persons basking betimes where terrace walls were warm, in the blue-frocked, brass-labelled official-ism of humble rakers and scrapers, in the deep references of a straight-pacing priest or the sharp ones of a white-gaitered, red-legged soldier. He watched little brisk figures, figures whose movement was as the tick of the great Paris clock, take their smooth diagonal from point to point; the air had a taste as of something mixed with art, something that pre-sented nature as a whitecapped master-*chef*. The palace was gone; Strether remembered the palace;

and when he gazed into the irremediable void of its site the historic sense in him might have been freely at play—the play under which in Paris indeed it so often winces like a touched nerve. He filled out spaces with dim symbols of scenes; he caught the gleam of white statues at the base of which, with his letters out, he could tilt back a straw-bottomed chair. But his drift was to the other side, and it floated him unspent up the Rue de Seine and as far as the Luxembourg gardens, where terraces, alleys, vistas, fountains, little trees in green tubs, little women in white caps and shrill little girls at play all sunnily "composing" together, he passed an hour in which the cup of his impressions truly overflowed.

The Ambassadors, 1903

"The great thing?"

"The sense of having done the best—the sense which is the real life of the artist and the absence of which is his death, of having drawn from his intellectual instrument the finest music that nature had hidden in it, of having played it as it should be played. He either does that or he doesn't—and if he doesn't he isn't worth speaking of. And precisely those who really know don't speak of him. He may still hear a great chatter, but what he hears most is the incorruptible silence of Fame."

Practically, Mrs. Varian's acquaintance with literature was confined to the *New York Interviewer*; as she very justly said, after you had read the *Interviewer*, you had no time for anything else.

MAY 3

One of these gaps in Mrs. Assingham's completeness was her want of children; the other was her want of wealth. It was wonderful how little either, in the fullness of time, came to show; sympathy and curiosity could render their objects practically filial, just as an English husband who in his military years had "run" everything in his regiment could make economy blossom like the rose.

MAY 4

At last the new voyagers began to emerge from below and to look about them vaguely, with the suspicious expression of face which is to be perceived in the newly embarked, and which, as directed to the receding land, resembles that of a person who begins to perceive himself the victim of a trick. Earth and ocean, in such glances, are made the subject of a general objection, and many travellers, in these circumstances, have an air at once duped and superior, which seems to say that they could easily go ashore if they would."

MAY 5

It has become the fashion to be effective at the expense of the sitter, to make some little point, or inflict some little dig, with a heated party air, rather than to catch a talent in the fact, follow its line and put a ringer on its essence: so that the exquisite art of criticism, smothered in grossness, finds itself turned into a question of "sides."

MAY 6
THE ALTAR OF THE DEAD, 1895

A woman when she was wronged was always more wronged than a man, and there were conditions when the least she could have got off with was more than the most he could have to endure.

MAY 7
BROWNING IN WESTMINSTER ABBEY, 1891

His voice sounds loudest, and also clearest, for the things that, as a race, we like best—the fascination of faith, the acceptance of life, the respect for its mysteries, the endurance of its charges, the vitality of the will, the validity of character, the beauty of action, the seriousness, above all, of the great human passion. If Browning had spoken for us in no other way, he ought to have been made sure of, tamed and chained as a classic, on account of the extraordinary beauty of his treatment of the special relation between man and woman.

MAY 8

THE PAPERS, 1903

Almost all they had with any security was their youth, complete, admirable, very nearly invulnerable, or as yet unattackable; for they didn't count their talent, which they had originally taken for granted and had since then lacked freedom of mind, as well indeed as any offensive reason, to reappraise.

MAY 9

THE MADONNA OF THE FUTURE, 1873

"You see I have the great advantage that I lose no time. These hours I spend with you are pure profit. They are *suggestive*! Just as the truly religious soul is always at worship, the genuine artist is always in labour. He takes his property wherever he finds it, and learns some precious secret from every object that stands up in the light. If you but knew the rapture of observation!"

MAY 10

THE WINGS OF THE DOVE, 1903

He had thought, no doubt, from the day he was born, much more than he had acted; except indeed that he remembered thoughts—a few of them—which at the moment of their coming to him had thrilled him almost like adventures.

MAY 11

THE MADONNA OF THE FUTURE, 1873

"I'm the half of a genius—where in the wide world is my other half? Lodged perhaps in the vulgar soul, the cunning, ready ringers of some dull copyist or some trivial artisan, who turns out by the dozen his easy prodigies of touch! But it's not for me to sneer at him, he at least does something. He's not a dawdler!"

MAY 12

There was at this season a wonderful month of May—as soft as a drop of the wind in a gale that had kept one awake.

MAY 13

EUGENE PICKERING, 1874

"I said just now I always supposed I was happy; it's true. But now that my eyes are open I see I was only stultified. I was like a poodle-dog that is led about by a blue ribbon, and scoured and combed and fed on slops. It wasn't life; life is learning to know oneself."

MAY 14

THE WINGS OF THE DOVE, 1903

It had a vulgar sound—as throughout in love, the names of things, the verbal terms of intercourse, were, compared with love itself, vulgar.

MAY 15
THE AWKWARD AGE, 1899

There hung about him still moreover the faded fragrance of the superstition that hospitality not declined is one of the things that "oblige." It obliged the thoughts, for Mr. Longdon, as well as the manners.

MAY 16
THE WINGS OF THE DOVE, 1903

A less vulgarly, a less obviously purchasing or parading person she couldn't have imagined; but it was all the same the truth of truths that the girl couldn't get away from her wealth. She might leave her conscientious companion as freely alone with it as possible and never ask a question, scarce even tolerate a reference; but it was in the fine folds of the helplessly expensive little black frock that she drew over the grass—it was in the curious and splendid coils of hair "done" with no eye whatever to the *mode du jour*, that peeped from under the corresponding indifference of her hat, the merely personal tradition that suggested a sort of noble inelegance. She couldn't dress it away, nor walk it away, nor read it away, nor think it away; she could neither smile it away in any dreamy absence, nor blow it away in any softened sigh. She couldn't have lost it if she had tried—that was what it was to be really rich. It had to be *the* thing you were.

MAY 17

The day was, even in the heart of London, of a rich, lowbrowed, weather-washed English type. So far as this was the case the impression of course could only be lost on a mere vague Italian; it was one of those things for which you had to be, blessedly, an American.

MAY 18

Nanda hovered there slim and charming, feathered and ribboned, dressed in thin, fresh fabrics and faint colors.

"Yes," Mrs. Brook resignedly mused; "you dress for yourself."

"Oh, how can you say that," the girl asked, "when I never stick in a pin but what I think of *you*?"

"Well," Mrs. Brook moralized, "one must always, I consider, think, as a sort of *point de repère*, of some one good person. Only it's best if it's a person one's afraid of. You do very well, but I'm not enough. What one really requires is a kind of salutary terror."

MAY 19

The nearest approach to anxiety indulged in as yet by the elder lady was on her taking occasion to wonder if what she had more than anything else got hold of mightn't be one of the finer, one of the finest, one of the rarest—as she called it so that she might call it nothing worse—cases of American intensity. Meanwhile, decidedly, it was enough that the girl was as charming as she was queer and as queer as she was charming—all of which was a rare amusement.

MAY 20

"Complete" is of course a great word, and there is no art at all, we are often reminded, that is not on too many sides an abject compromise. The element of compromise is always there; it is of the essence; we live with it, and it may serve to keep us humble. The formula of the whole matter is sufficiently expressed perhaps in a reply I found myself once making to an inspired but discouraged friend, a fellow-craftsman who had declared in his despair that there was no use trying, that it [the novel] was a form absolutely too difficult. "Too difficult indeed; yet there is one way to master it—which is to pretend consistently that it isn't."

MAY 21

Love demands certain things as a right; but Catherine had no sense of her rights; she had only a consciousness of immense and unexpected favours. Her very gratitude for these things had hushed itself, as it seemed to her there would be something of impudence in making a festival of her secret.

MAY 22

There were ten days left of the beautiful month of May—the most precious month of all to the true Rome-lover. The sky was a blaze of blue, and the plash of the fountains, in their mossy niches, had lost its chill and doubled its music. On the corners of the warm, bright streets one stumbled upon bundles of flowers.

MAY 23

There was something in Miss Stackpole he had begun to like; it seemed to him that if she was not a charming woman she was at least a very good fellow.

She was wanting in distinction, but, as Isabel had said, she was brave, and one never quite saw the end of the value of that.

MAY 24

THE GOLDEN BOWL, 1904

His life would be full of machinery, which was the antidote to superstition; which was, in its turn, too much the consequence, or at least the exhalation, of archives.

MAY 25

EMERTON, 1887

We have the impression, somehow, that life had never bribed him to look at anything but the soul; and indeed in the world in which he grew up and lived the bribes and lures, the beguilements and prizes, were few. He was in an admirable position for showing, what he constantly endeavored to show, that the prize was within.

MAY 26

"You think we can escape disagreeable duties by taking romantic views—that is your great illusion, my dear. But we can't. You must be prepared on many occasions in life to please no-one at all—not even yourself."

MAY 27
THE GOLDEN BOWL, 1904

It fell in easily with the tenderness of her disposition to remember she might occasionally make him happy by an intimate confidence. This was one of her rules—full as she was of little rules, considerations, provisions.

MAY 28
THE AWKWARD AGE, 1899

"I never really have believed in the existence of friendship in big societies—in great towns and great crowds. It's a plant that takes time and space and air; and London society is a huge 'squash,' as we elegantly call it—an elbowing, pushing, perspiring, chattering mob."

"Oh, your friend's a type, the grand old American—what shall one call it? The Hebrew prophet, Ezekiel, Jeremiah, who used when I was a little girl, in the rue Montaigne, to come to see my father, and who was usually the American minister to the Tuileries or some other court. I haven't seen one these ever so many years; the sight of it warms my poor old chilled heart; this specimen is wonderful."

MAY 30

JAMES RUSSELL LOWELL, 1891

To me, at any rate, there is something seductive in the way in which, in the Harvard "Commemoration Ode," for instance, the air of the study mingles with the hot breath of passion. The reader who is eternally bribed by form may ask himself whether Mr. Lowell's prose or his poetry has the better chance of a long life—the hesitation being justified by the rare degree in which the prose has the great qualities of style; but in the presence of some of the splendid stanzas inspired by the war-time (and among them I include, of course, the second series of "The Biglow Papers") one feels that, whatever shall become of the essays, the transmission from generation to generation of such things as these may safely be left to the national conscience.

[*DECORATION DAY*]

MAY 31

PANDORA, 1854

There appeared now to be a constant danger of marrying the American girl; it was something one had to reckon with, like the rise in prices, the telephone, the discovery of dynamite, the Chassepot rifle, the socialistic spirit; it was one of the complications of modern life.

JUNE

The lower windows of the great white house, which
stood high and square, opened to a wide flagged
terrace, the parapet of which, an old balustrade of
stone, was broken in the middle of its course by a
flight of stone steps that descended to a wonderful
garden. The terrace had the afternoon shade and
fairly hung over the prospect that dropped away and
circled it—the prospect, beyond the series of gardens, of scattered, splendid trees and green glades,
an horizon mainly of woods. Nanda Brookenham,
one day at the end of July, coming out to find the
place unoccupied as yet by other visitors, stood
there awhile with an air of happy possession. She
moved from end to end of the terrace, pausing, gaz-
ing about her, taking in with a face that showed the
pleasure of a brief independence the combination
of delightful things—of old rooms with old decora-
tions that gleamed and gloomed through the high
windows, of old gardens that squared themselves
in the wide angles of old walls, of wood-walks rus-
tling in the afternoon breeze and stretching away to
further reaches of solitude and summer. The scene
had an expectant stillness that she was too charmed
to desire to break; she watched it, listened to it, fol-

lowed with her eyes the white butterflies among the flowers below her, then gave a start as the cry of a peacock came to her from an unseen alley.

The Awkward Age, 1904

୧ଚ ଚ୨

JUNE 1

To deny the relevancy of subject-matter and the importance of the moral quality of a work of art strikes us as, in two words, very childish. We do not know what the great moralists would say about the matter—they would probably treat it very good-humouredly; but that is not the question. There is very little doubt what the great artists would say. People of that temper feel that the whole thinking man is one, and that to count out the moral element in one's appreciation of an artistic total is exactly as sane as it would be (if the total were a poem) to eliminate all the words in three syllables, or to consider only such portions of it as had been written by candle-light.

JUNE 2

"The fact is I've been comfortable so many years that I suppose I've got so used to it I don't know it."
"Yes, that's the bore of comfort," said Lord Warburton, "We only know when we're uncomfortable."

JUNE 3

He had perceived on the spot that any serious discussion of veracity, of loyalty, or rather of the want of them, practically took her unprepared, as if it were quite new to her. He had noticed it before: it was the English, the American sign that duplicity, like "love," had to be joked about. It couldn't be "gone into."

JUNE 4

The boulevard was all alive, brilliant with illuminations, with the variety and gaiety of the crowd, the dazzle of shops and cafes seen through uncovered fronts or immense lucid plates, the flamboyant porches of theatres and the flashing lamps of carriages, the far-spreading murmur of talkers and strollers, the uproar of pleasure and prosperity, the general magnificence of Paris on a perfect evening in June.

JUNE 5

"Well, that's what struck me as especially nice, or rather as very remarkable in her—her being, with all her attraction, one of the obscure seventy millions; a mere little almost nameless tossed-up flower out of the mixed lap of the great American people. I mean for the charming person she is. I doubt if, after all, any other huge mixed lap—"

"Yes, if she were English, on those lines, one wouldn't look at her, would one? I say, fancy her English."

JUNE 6

THE REVERBERATOR, 1888

A fate was rather a cumbersome and formidable possession, which it relieved her that some kind person should undertake the keeping of.

JUNE 7

THE AUTHOR OF BELTRAFFIO, 1885

That was the way many things struck me at that time in England; as if they were reproductions of something that existed primarily in art or literature. It was not the picture, the poem, the Active page that seemed to me a copy; these things were the originals, and the life of happy and distinguished people was fashioned in their image.

JUNE 8
THE AWKWARD AGE, 1899

She had sunk down upon the bench almost with a sense of adventure, yet, not too fluttered to wonder if it wouldn't have been nappy to bring a book; the charm of which, precisely, would have been in feeling everything about her too beautiful to let her read.

JUNE 9
GUY DE MAUPASSANT, 1888

When it is a question of an artistic process we must always distrust very sharp distinctions, for there is surely in every living method a little of every other method.

JUNE 10
CHARLES BAUDELAIRE, 1878

People of a large taste prefer rich works to poor ones and they are not inclined to assent to the assumption that the process is the whole work. We are safe in believing that all this is comfortably clear to most of those who have, in any degree, been initiated into art by production. For them the subject is as much a part of their work as their hunger is a part of their dinner. Baudelaire was not so far from being of this way of thinking as some of his admirers would persuade us; yet we may say on the whole that he was the victim of a grotesque illusion. He tried to make fine verses on ignoble subjects, and in our opinion he signally failed. He gives, as a poet, a perpetual impression of discomfort and pain. He went in search of corruption, and the ill-conditioned jade proved a thankless muse. The thinking reader, feeling himself, as a critic, all one, as we have said, finds the beauty nullified by the ugliness.

JUNE 11

THE PRINCESS CASAMASSIMA, 1886

"And indeed I have spoken just *because* the air is sweet, and the place ornamental, and the day a holiday, and your company exhilarating. All this has had the effect that an object has if you plunge it into a cup of water—the water overflows."

JUNE 12

EUGENE PICKERING, 1874

His mind was admirably active, and always, after an hour's talk with him, I asked myself what experience could really do, that innocence hadn't done to make it bright and fine.

JUNE 13

Of course, furthermore, "it took" in particular "our set," with its positive child-terror of the *banal*, to be either so foolish or so wise; though indeed I've never quite known where our set begins and ends, and have had to content myself on this score with the indication once given me by a lady next whom I was placed at dinner: "Oh, it's bounded on the north by Ibsen and on the south by Sargent."

JUNE 14

There was a fresco of Guercino, to which Rowland, though he had seen it on his former visit to Rome, went dutifully to pay his respects. But Roderick, though he had never seen it, declared that it couldn't be worth a fig, and that he didn't care to look at ugly things. He remained stretched on his overcoat, which he had spread on the grass, while Rowland went off envying the intellectual comfort of genius which can arrive at serene conclusions without disagreeable processes.

JUNE 15

THE BOSTONIANS, 1886

Miss Birdseye's voice expressed only the cheerful weariness which had marked all this last period of her life, and which seemed to make it now as blissful as it was suitable that she should pass away. There was, to Ransom something almost august in the trustful renunciation of her countenance; something in it seemed to say that she had been ready long before, but as the time was not ripe she had waited, with her usual faith that all was for the best; only, at present, since the right conditions met, she couldn't help feeling that it was quite a luxury, the greatest she had ever tasted.

JUNE 16

THE WINGS OF THE DOVE, 1903

"One could almost pity him—he has had such a good conscience." "That's exactly the inevitable ass." "Yes, but it wasn't—I could see from the only few things she first told me—that he meant *her* the least harm. He intended none whatever."

"That's always the ass at his worst."

JUNE 17

THE AMBASSADORS, 1903

It must be added, however, that, thanks to his constant habit of shaking the bottle in which life handed him the wine of experience, he presently found the taste of the lees, rising, as usual, into his draught.

JUNE 18

THE WINGS OF THE DOVE, 1903

Their feeling was—or at any rate their modest general plea—that there was no place they would have liked to go to; there was only the sense of finding they liked, wherever they were, the place to which they had been brought.

JUNE 19

GEORGE SAND, 1878

On one side an extraordinary familiarity with the things of the mind, the play of character, the psychological mystery, and a beautiful clearness and quietness, a beautiful instinct of justice in dealing with them; on the other side a startling absence of delicacy, of reticence, of the sense of certain spiritual sanctities and reserves.

Excitement, for each of them had naturally dropped, and—what they had left behind, or tried to, the great serious facts of life—were once more coming into sight as objects loom through smoke when smoke begins to clear.

JUNE 21

RODERICK HUDSON, 1875

Rowland watched the shadows on Mount Holyoke, listened to the gurgle of the river, and sniffed the balsam of the pines. A gentle breeze had begun to tickle their summits, and brought the smell of the mown grass across from the elm-dotted river meadows. It seemed to him beautiful, and suddenly a strange feeling of prospective regret took possession of him. Something seemed to tell him that later, in a foreign land, he should remember it with longing and regret.

"It's a wretched business," he said, "this virtual quarrel of ours with our own country, this everlasting impatience to get out of it. Is one's only safety then in flight? This is an American day, an American landscape, an American atmosphere. It certainly has its merits, and some time when I am shivering with ague in classic Italy I shall accuse myself of having slighted them."

JUNE 22

She was none the less plucky for being at bottom a shameless Philistine, ambitious of a front garden with rockwork; and she presented the plebeian character in none the less plastic a form.

JUNE 23

They wandered along the rocky waterside to a rocky shrub-covered point, which made a walk of just the right duration. Here all the homely languor of the region, the mild, fragrant Cape quality, the sweetness of white sands, quiet waters, low promontories where there were paths amid the barberries and tidal pools gleamed in the sunset —here all the spirit of a ripe summer afternoon seemed to hang in the air. There were wood-walks too; they sometimes followed bosky uplands, where accident had grouped the trees with odd effects of "style," and where in grassy intervals and fragrant nooks of rest they came out upon sudden patches of Arcady.

JUNE 24

THE PORTRAIT OF A LADY, 1881

A dissatisfied mind, whatever else it lack, is rarely in want of reasons; they bloom as thick as butterflies in June.

JUNE 25

RODERICK HUDSON, 1875

Gloriani with his head on one side, pulling his long moustache and looking keenly from half-closed eyes at the lighted marble, represented art with a worldly motive, skill unleavened by faith, the mere base maximum of cleverness.

JUNE 26

THE AMBASSADORS, 1903

"You're being used for a thing you ain't fit for. People don't take a fine-tooth comb to groom a horse,"

"Am I a fine-tooth comb." Strether laughed. "It's something I never called myself!"

"It's what you are, all the same. You ain't so young as you were, but you've kept your teeth."

JUNE 27

She was passively comical—a person whom people, to make talk lively, described to each other and imitated.

JUNE 28

It gave her, nevertheless, a pleasure that had some of the charm of unwontedness to feel, with that admirable keenness with which she was capable of feeling things, that he had a disposition without any edges; that even his humorous. irony always softened toward the point.

JUNE 29

A person who knew him well would, if present at the scene, have found occasion in it to be freshly aware that he was, in his quiet way, master of two distinct kinds of urbanity, the kind that added to distance and the kind that diminished it.

"He lived and moved altogether in. his own little province of art. A creature more unsullied by the world it is impossible to conceive, and I often thought it a flaw in his artistic character that he had not a harmless vice or two. It amused me greatly at times to think that he was of our shrewd Yankee race; but, after all, there could be no better token of his American origin than this high aesthetic fever. The very heat of his devotion was a sign of conversion; those born to European opportunity manage better to reconcile enthusiasm with comfort."

JULY

We kept to the fields and copses and commons, and breathed the same sweet air as the nibbling donkeys and the browsing sheep, whose woolliness seemed to me, in those early days of my acquaintance with English objects, but a part of the general texture of the small dense landscape, which looked as if the harvest were gathered by the shears. Everything was full of expression—from the big, bandy-legged geese, whose whiteness was a "note," amid all the tones of green, as they wandered beside a neat little oval pool, the foreground of a thatched and white-washed inn, with a grassy approach and a pictorial sign—from these humble wayside animals to the crest of high woods which let a gable or a pinnacle peep here and there, and looked, even at a distance, like trees of good company, conscious of an individual profile. I admired the hedge-rows, I plucked the faint-hued heather, and I was forever stopping to say how charming I thought the thread-like foot paths across the fields, which wandered in a diagonal of finer grain, from one smooth tile to another. We sat and smoked upon stiles, broaching paradoxes in the decent English air, we took short cuts across a park or two, where the bracken was deep, and my companion nodded to the old woman at the gate. We skirted rank covers, which rustled here and there as we passed, and we stretched ourselves at last on a heathery hillside where, if the sun was not too hot, neither was the earth too cold, and where the country lay beneath us in a rich blue mist.

The Author of Beltraffio, 1885

෨෧෧ඁ

THE EUROPEANS, 1878

"You strike me as very capable of enjoying, if the chance were given you, and yet at the same time as incapable of wrong-doing."

"What ought one to do? To give parties, to go to the theatre, to read novels, to keep late hours?"

"I don't think it's what one does or doesn't do that promotes enjoyment," her companion answered.

"It is the general way of looking at life."

"They look at it as a discipline—that is what they do here. I have often been told that."

"Well, that's very good. But there is another way—to look at it as an opportunity."

THE GOLDEN BOWL, 1904

He knew his ante natal history, knew it in every detail, and it was a thing to keep causes well before him. What was his frank judgment of so much of its ugliness, he asked himself, but a part of the cultivation of humility? If what had come to him wouldn't do he must *make* something different.

"Some things—some differences—are felt, not learned. To you liberty is not natural; you are like a person who has bought a repeater and in his satisfaction, is constantly making it sound. To a real American girl her liberty is a very vulgarly ticking old clock."

JULY 4

CHARLES BAUDELAIRE, 1878

He knew evil not by experience, not as something within himself, but by contemplation and curiosity, as something outside of himself, by which his own intellectual agility was not in the least discomposed, rather, indeed (as we say his fancy was of a dusky cast) agreeably flattered and stimulated. In the former case, Baudelaire, with his other gifts, might have been a great poet. But, as it is, evil for him begins outside and not inside, and consists primarily of a great deal of lurid landscape and unclean furniture. This is an almost ludicrously puerile view of the matter—a good way to embrace Baudelaire at a glance is to say that he was, in his treatment of evil, exactly what Hawthorne was not—Hawthorne, who felt the thing at its source, deep in the human consciousness. Baudelaire's infinitely slighter volume of genius apart, he was a sort of Hawthorne reversed.

[NATHANIEL HAWTHORNE BORN ON THIS DAY IN 1804]

JULY 5

THE GOLDEN BOWL 1904

For it may immediately be mentioned that this amiable man bethought himself of his personal advantage, in general, only when it might appear to him that other advantages, those of other persons, had successfully put in their claim. It may be mentioned also that he always figured other persons—such was the law of his nature—as a numerous array.

JULY 6

AN INTERNATIONAL EPISODE, 1879

"I must say I think that when one goes to a foreign country, one ought to enjoy the differences. Of course there are differences; otherwise what did one come abroad for?"

JULY 7

In the long afternoons, of which the length was but the measure of her gratified eagerness, they took a boat on the river, the dear little river, as Isabel called it, where the opposite shore seemed still a part of the foreground of the landscape; or drove over the country in a phaeton—a low, capacious, thick-wheeled phaeton. Isabel enjoyed it largely, and, handling the reins in a manner which approved itself to the groom as "knowing," was never weary of driving her uncle's capital horses through winding lawns and byways full of the rural incidents she had confidently expected to find; past cottages thatched and timbered, past ale-houses latticed and sanded, past patches of ancient common and glimpses of empty parks, between hedgerows made thick by midsummer.

JULY 8

To what degree a purpose in a work of art is a source of corruption I shall not attempt to enquire; the one that seems to me least dangerous is the purpose of making a perfect work.

She knew governesses were poor; Miss Overmore was unmentionably and Mrs. Wix familiarly so. Neither this, however, nor the old brown frock, nor the diadem, nor the button, made a difference for Maisie in the charm put forth through everything, the charm of Mrs. Wix's conveying that somehow, in her ugliness and her poverty, she was peculiarly and soothingly safe, safer than anyone in the world— than papa, than mamma, than the lady with the arched eyebrows; safer even, though much less beautiful, than Miss Overmore, on whose loveliness, as she supposed it, the little girl was faintly conscious that one couldn't rest with quite the same tucked-in and kissed for good-night feeling. Mrs. Wix was as safe as Clara Matilda, who was in heaven, and yet, embarrassingly, also in Kensal Green, where they had been together to see her little huddled grave.

Like all men of a large pattern, he was composed of many different pieces; and what was always striking in him was the mixture of simplicity with the fruit of the most various observation.

JULY 11

Women have no faculty of imagination with regard to a man's work beyond a vague idea that it doesn't matter.

JULY 12

One could trust him, at any rate, round all the corners of the world; and, withal, he was not absolutely simple, which would have been excess; he was only relatively simple.

JULY 13

Olive had seen how Verena was moved by Miss Birdseye's death; how at the sight of that unique woman's majestically simple withdrawal from a scene in which she had held every vulgar aspiration, every worldly standard and lure, so cheap, the girl had been touched again with the spirit of their most confidant hours, had flamed up with the faith that no narrow personal joy could compare in sweetness with the idea of doing something for those who had always suffered and who waited still.

JULY 14

"There it is. The thing's so perfect that it's open to as many interpretations as any other great work—a poem of Goethe, a dialogue of Plato, a symphony of Beethoven. "It simply stands quiet, you mean," Sam said, "and lets us call it names?" "Yes, but all such loving ones."

JULY 15

"But what you say," she said at last, "means *change*!"
"Change for the better!" cried Rowland.
"How can one tell? As one stands one knows the worst. It seems to me very frightful to develop."
"One is in for it in one way or another, and one might as well do it with a good grace as with a bad! Since one can't escape life it is better to take it by the hand."

JULY 16

It had never been pride, Maud Manningham, had hinted, that kept *her* from crying when other things made for it; it had only been that these same things, at such times, made still more for business, arrangements, correspondence, the ringing of bells, the marshalling of servants, the taking of decisions. "I might be crying now," she said, "if I weren't writing letters."

JULY 17

THE LESSON OF THE MASTER, 1892

He saw more in his face, and he liked it the better for its not telling its whole story in the first three minutes. That story came out as one read, in short instalments.

JULY 18

WASHINGTON SQUARE, 1881

In a country in which, to play a social part, you must either earn your income or make believe that you earn it, the healing art has appeared in a high degree to combine the two recognized sources of credit. It belongs to the realm of the practical, which in the United States is a great recommendation; and it is touched by the light of science—a merit appreciated in a community in which the love of knowledge has not always been accompanied by leisure and opportunity.

JULY 19

The thick warm air of a London July floated beneath them, suffused with the everlasting uproar of the town, which appeared to have sunk into quietness but again became a mighty voice as soon as one listened for it; here and there, in poor windows, glimmered a turbid light, and high above, in a clearer, smokeless zone, a sky still fair and luminous, a faint silver star looked down. The sky was the same that, far away, in the country, bent over golden fields and purple hills and copses where nightingales sang; but from this point of view everything that covered the earth was ugly and sordid, and seemed to express or to represent the weariness of toil.

JULY 20

What held them together was in short that they were in the same boat, a cockle-shell in a great rough sea, and that the movements required for keeping it afloat were not only what the situation safely permitted but also made for reciprocity and safety.

"The crop we gather depends upon the seed we sow. He may be the biggest genius of the age; his potatoes won't come up without his hoeing them. If he takes things so almighty easy as—well, as one or two young fellows of genius I've had under my eye—his produce will never gain the prize. Take the word for it of a man who has made his way inch by inch and doesn't believe that we wake up to find our work done because we have lain all night a dreaming of it; any thing worth doing is devilish hard to do! If your young gentleman finds things easy and has a good time of it and says he likes the life, it's a sign that—as I may say—you had better step round to the office and look at the books."

JULY 22

THE PRINCESS CASAMASSIMA, 1886

At the thought of her limited, stinted life, the patient, humdrum effort of her needle and scissors, which had ended only in a showroom where there was nothing to show and a pensive reference to the cut of sleeves no longer worn, the tears again rose to his eyes.

JULY 23

"He's full of stuff—there's a great deal of him, too much to come out all at once. He has ability, he has ideas; he has absolute honesty; and he has moreover a good stiff back of his own. He's a fellow of head; he's a fellow of heart—in short he's a man of gold.

JULY 24

THE GOLDEN BOWL, 1904

"Beyond giving her credit for everything, it's none of my business."

"I don't see how you can give credit without knowing the facts."

"Can't I give it generally—for dignity? Dignity I mean, in misfortune."

"You've got to postulate the misfortune first."

"Well," said Maggie, "I can do that. Isn't it always a misfortune to be—when you're so fine—so wasted? And yet," she went on, "not to wail about it, not to look even as if you knew it?"

JULY 25

Nothing in him was more amiable than the terms maintained between the rigor of his personal habits and his free imagination of the habits of others.

JULY 26

"The curious thing is that the more the mind takes in, the more it has space for, and that all one's ideas are like the Irish people at home who live in the different corners of a room and take boarders."

JULY 27

It was nothing new to him, however, as we know, that a man might have—at all events such a man as *he* was—an amount of experience out of any proportion to his adventures.

JULY 28

This was the real thing; the real thing was to be quite away from the pompous roads, well within the centre and on the stretches of shabby grass. Here were benches and smutty sheep; here were idle lads at games of ball, with their cries mild in the thick air; here were wanderers, anxious and tired like herself; here doubtless were hundreds of others just in the same box.

JULY 29

"You can't make of a silk purse a sow's ear! It's grievous indeed if you like—there are people who can't be vulgar for trying. *He* can't—it wouldn't come off, I promise you, even once. It takes more than trying—it comes by grace."

JULY 30

Her head, extremely fair and exquisitely festal, was like a happy fancy, a notion of the antique, on an old precious medal, some silver coin of the Renaissance; while her slim lightness and brightness, her gayety, her expression, her decision, contributed to an effect that might have been felt by a poet as half mythological and half conventional. He could have compared her to a goddess still partly engaged in a morning cloud, or to a sea-nymph waist high in the summer surge.

JULY 31

THE AWKWARD AGE, 1899

Mr. Longdon's smile was beautiful—it supplied so many meanings that when presently he spoke he seemed already to have told half his story.

AUGUST

The ripeness of summer lay upon the land, and yet there was nothing in the country Basil Ransom traversed that seemed of maturity; nothing but the apples in the little tough dense orchards which gave a suggestion of sour fruition here and there, and the tall, bright golden-rod at the bottom of the bare stone dykes. There were no fields of yellow grain; only here and there a crop of brown hay. But there was a kind of soft scrubbiness in the landscape, and a sweetness begotten of low horizons, of mild air, with a possibility of summer haze, of unguarded inlets where on August mornings the water must be brightly blue. He liked the very smell of the soil as he wandered along; cool, soft whiffs of evening met him at bends of the road which disclosed very little more—unless it might be a band of straight-stemmed woodland, keeping, a little, the red glow from the west, or (as he went further) an old house shingled all over, gray and slightly collapsing, which looked down at him from a steep bank, at the top of wooden steps. He was already refreshed; he had tasted the breath of nature, measured his long grind in New York without a vacation, with the repetition of the daily movement up and down the long, straight, maddening city, like a bucket in a well or a shuttle in a loom.

The Bostonians, 1886

✧

AUGUST 1

"I've touched a thousand things, but which one of them have I turned into gold? The artist has to do only with that—he knows nothing of any baser metal."

AUGUST 2

It had rained heavily in the night, and though the pavements were now dry, thanks to a cleansing breeze, the August morning, with its hovering, thick-drifting clouds and freshened air, was cool and grey. The multitudinous green of the Park had been deepened, and a wholesome smell of irrigation, purging the place of dust and of odours less acceptable, rose from the earth.

AUGUST 3

The novelist who leaves the extraordinary out of his account is liable to awkward confrontations, as we are compelled to reflect in this age of newspapers and of universal publicity. The next report of the next divorce case (to give an instance) shall offer us a picture of astounding combinations of circumstance and behaviour, and the annals of any energetic race are rich in curious anecdote and startling example.

AUGUST 4

The world was, first and foremost, for George Eliot, the moral, the intellectual world; the personal spectacle came after; and lovingly, humanly as she regarded it we constantly feel that she cares for the things she finds in it only so far as they are types. The philosophic door is always open, on her stage, and we are aware that the somewhat cooling draught of ethical purpose draws across it.

AUGUST 5

He felt his own holiday so successfully large and free that he was full of allowances and charities in respect to those cabined and confined: his instinct towards a spirit so strapped down as Waymarsh's was to walk round it on tiptoe for fear of waking it up to a sense of losses by this time irretrievable.

AUGUST 6

He knew the small vista of her street, closed at the end and as dreary as an empty pocket, where the pairs of shabby little houses, semi-detached but indissolubly united, were like married couples on bad terms.

AUGUST 7

She liked almost everything, including the English rain. "There is always a little of it, and never too much at once," she said; "and it never wets you, and it always smells good." She declared that in England the pleasures of smell were great—that in this inimitable island there was a certain mixture of fog and beer and soot which, however odd it might sound, was the national aroma, and most agreeable to the nostril.

AUGUST 8

"Try to do some really good work."
"Oh I want to, heaven knows!"
"Well, you can't do it without sacrifices; don't believe

that for a moment," said Henry St. George. "I've made none. I've had everything. In other words, I've missed everything."

AUGUST 9

THE LESSON OF THE MASTER, 1892

"One would like to paint such a girl as that," Overt continued.

Ah, there it is—there's nothing like life! When you're finished, squeezed dry and used up and you think the sack's empty, you're still spoken to, you still get touches and thrills, the idea springs up—out of the lap of the actual—and shows you there's always something to be done."

AUGUST 10

THE PRINCESS CASAMASSIMA, 1886

Miss Pynsent couldn't embrace the state of mind of people who didn't apologize, though she vaguely envied and admired it, she herself spending much of her time in making excuses for obnoxious acts she had not committed.

AUGUST 11

EUGENE PICKERING, 1874

"I find I'm an active, sentient, intelligent creature, with desires, with passions, with possible convictions,— even with what I never dreamed of, a possible will of my own! I find there is a world to know, a life to lead, men and women to form a thousand relations with. It all lies there like a great surging sea, where we must plunge and dive and feel the breeze and breast the waves. I stand shivering here on the brink, staring, longing, wondering, charmed by the smell of the brine and yet afraid of the water."

AUGUST 12

JAMES RUSSELL LOWELL, 1891

After a man's long work is over and the sound of his voice is still, those in whose regard he has held a high place find his image strangely simplified and summarized. The hand of death in passing over it, has smoothed the folds, made it more typical and general. The figure retained by the memory is compressed and intensified; accidents have dropped away from it and shades have ceased to count; it stands, sharply, for a few estimated and cherished things, rather than, nebulously, for a swarm of possibilities.

AUGUST 13

She was in short a most comfortable, profitable, agreeable person to live with. If for Isabel she had a fault it was that she was not natural; by which the girl meant, not that she was affected or pretentious, for from these vulgar vices no woman could have been more exempt; but that her nature had been too much overlaid by custom and her angles too much smoothed. She had become too flexible, too supple; she was too finished, too civilized. She was, in a word, too perfectly the social animal that man and woman are supposed to have been intended to be; and she had rid herself of every remnant of that tonic wildness which we may assume to have belonged even to the most amiable persons in the ages before country-house life was the fashion.

AUGUST 14

There were certain afternoons in August, long, beautiful and terrible, when one felt that the summer was rounding its curve, and the rustle of the full-leaved trees in the slanting golden light, in the breeze that ought to be delicious, seemed the voice of the coming autumn, of the warnings and dangers of life.

AUGUST 15

She wrote short stories, and she fondly believed she had her "note," the art of showing New England without showing it wholly in the kitchen.

AUGUST 16

And he gave Rowland to understand that he meant to live freely and largely and be as interested as occasion demanded. Rowland saw no reason to regard this as a menace of grossness, because in the first place there was in all dissipation, refine it as one might, a vulgarity which would disqualify it for Roderick's favour; and because in the second the young sculptor was a man to regard all things in the light of his art, to hand over his passions to his genius to be dealt with, and to find that he could live largely enough without exceeding the circle of pure delights.

AUGUST 17

She summed up the sociable, humorous, ignorant chatter of the masses, their capacity for offensive and defensive passion, their instinctive perception of their strength on the day they should really exercise it; and, as much as any of this, their ideal of something snug and prosperous, where washed hands and plates in rows on dressers, and stuffed birds under glass, and family photographs, would symbolize success.

AUGUST 18

THE GOLDEN BOWL, 1901

Besides, who but himself really knew what *he*, after all, hadn't, or even had, gained? The beauty of her condition was keeping him, at any rate, as he might feel, in sight of the sea, where, though his personal dips were over, the whole thing could shine at him, and the air and the plash and the play become for him too a sensation. That couldn't be fixed upon him as missing; since if it wasn't personally floating, if it wasn't even sitting in the sand, it could yet pass very well for breathing the bliss, in a communicated irresistible way—for tasting the balm.

AUGUST 19

The great church had no altar for his worship, no direct voice for his soul: but it was none the less soothing even to sanctity; for he could feel while there what he couldn't elsewhere, that he was a plain tired man taking the holiday he had earned.

AUGUST 20

"After all, the opinions of our friends are not what we love them for, and therefore I don't see why they should be what we hate them for."

AUGUST 21

The near view of the big queer country had at last, this summer, imposed itself: so many other men had got it and were making it, in talk, not only a convenience but a good deal of a nuisance, that it appeared to have become, defensively, as necessary as the electric light in the flat one might wish to let;

as to which, the two friends, after their ten bustling weeks, had now in fact grown to feel that they could press the American button with the best.

AUGUST 22

RODERICK HUDSON, 1875

"Do you know I sometimes think I'm a man of genius, half finished? The genius has been left out, the faculty of expression is wanting; but the need for expression remains, and I spend my days groping for the latch of a closed door."

AUGUST 23

THE MADONNA OF THE FUTURE, 1873

"There is only one Raphael, but an artist may still be an artist; the days of illumination are gone; visions are rare; we have to look long to see them. But in meditation we may still cultivate the ideal; round it, smooth it, perfect it. The result certainly may be less than this; but still it may be good, it may be *great*!—it may hang somewhere, in after years, in goodly company, and keep the artist's memory warm. Think of being known to mankind after some such fashion as this! suspended here through the slow centuries in the gaze of an altered world; living on and on in the cunning of an eye and hand that are part of the dust of ages, a delight and a law to remote generations; making beauty a force and purity an example!"

AUGUST 24

THE PORTRAIT OF A LADY, 1881

"I judge more than I used to,—but it seems to me that I have earned the right. One can't judge till one is forty; before that we are too eager, too hard, too cruel, and in addition too ignorant."

AUGUST 25

THE WINGS OF THE DOVE, 1903

She had stature without height, grace without motion, presence without mass. Slender and simple, frequently soundless, she was somehow always in the line of the eye—she counted singularly for its pleasure. More "dressed," often with fewer accessories, than other women, or less dressed, should occasion require, with more, she probably couldn't have given the key to these felicities.

AUGUST 26

He walked and walked as if to show himself how little he had now to do; he had nothing to do but turn off to some hillside, where he might stretch himself and hear the poplar's rustle, and whence— in the course of an afternoon so spent, an afternoon richly suffused, too, with the sense of a book in his pocket—he should sufficiently command the scene to be able to pick out just the right little rustic inn for an experiment in respect to dinner.

AUGUST 27

His private invitation produced a kind of cheerful glow in regard to Mr. Dosson and Delia, whom he couldn't defend nor lucidly explain nor make people like, but whom he had ended, after so many days of familiar intercourse, by liking extremely himself. The way to get on with them—it was an immense simplification—was just to love them; one could do that even if one couldn't talk with them.

AUGUST 28

"Nothing is more charming than suddenly to come across something sharp and fresh after we've thought there was nothing more that could draw from us a groan. We've supposed we've had it all, have squeezed the last impression out of the last disappointment, penetrated to the last familiarity in the last surprise; then some fine day we find that we haven't done justice to life. There are little things that pop up and make us feel again. What *may* happen is after all incalculable. There's just a little chuck of the dice, and for three minutes we win."

AUGUST 29

She always ended, however, by feeling that having a charming surface doesn't necessarily prove that one is superficial.

AUGUST 30

Disappointment and despair were in such relations contagious, and there was clearly as much less again left to her as the little that was left to him. He showed her, laughing at the long queerness of it, how awfully little, as they called it, this was. He let it all come, but with more mirth than misery, and with a final abandonment of pride that was like changing at the end of a dreadful day from tight boots to slippers.

AUGUST 31

A LANDSCAPE PAINTER, 1866

"How can a man be simple and natural who's known to have a large income? That's the supreme curse. It's bad enough to have it; to be known to have it, to be known only because you have it, is most damnable."

SEPTEMBER

I woke up, by a quick transition, in the New Hamp-
shire mountains, in the deep valleys and the wide
woodlands, on the forest-fringed slopes, the far-
seeing crests of the high places, and by the side
of the liberal streams and the lonely lakes; things
full, at first, of the sweetness of belated recognition,
that of the sense of some bedimmed summer of the
distant prime flushing back into life and asking to
give again as much as possible of what it had given
before. There hung over these things the insistent
hush of a September Sunday morning. I went down
into the valley—that was an impression to woo by
stages; I walked beside one of those great fields of
standing Indian-corn which make, to the eye, so
perfect a note for the rest of the American rural
picture, throwing the conditions back as far as our
past permits, rather than forward, as so many other
things do, into the age to come. The maker of these
reflections betook himself at last, in any case, to an
expanse of rock by a large bend of the Saco, and
lingered there under the infinite charm of the place.
The rich, full lapse of the river, the perfect brown-
ness, clear and deep, as of liquid agate, in its wide

swirl, the large indifferent ease in its pace and motion, as of some great benevolent institution working smoothly; all this, with the sense of the deepening autumn about, gave I scarce know what pastoral nobleness to the scene, something raising it out of the reach of even the most restless of analysts. The analyst in fact could scarce be restless here; the impression, so strong and so final, persuaded him perfectly to peace. This, on September Sunday mornings, was what American beauty *should* be.

New England: An Autumn Impression, 1905

SEPTEMBER 1

GUY DE MAUPASSANT, 1888

It is as difficult to describe an action without glancing at its motive, its moral history, as it is to describe a motive without glancing at its practical consequence.

SEPTEMBER 2

THE AMBASSADORS, 1903

It would doubtless be difficult to-day—to name her and place her; she would certainly show, on knowledge, Miss Gostrey felt, as one of those convenient types who didn't keep you explaining—minds with doors as numerous as the many-tongued cluster of confessionals at St. Peter's.

SEPTEMBER 3

THE AUTHOR OF BELTRAFFIO, 1903

"When I see the kind of things that life does I despair of ever catching her peculiar trick. She has an impudence, life! If one risked a fiftieth part of the effects she risks! It takes ever so long to believe it. You don't know yet, my dear fellow. It isn't till one has been watching her for forty years that one finds out half of what she's up to! Therefore one's earlier things must inevitably contain a mass of rot."

SEPTEMBER 4

THE GOLDEN BOWL, 1904

"It only meant that there are perhaps better things to be done with Miss Stant than to criticise her. When once you begin *that* with anyone—!" He was vague and kind.

"I quite agree that it's better to keep out of it as long as one can. But when one *must* do it—"

"Yes?" he asked as she paused.

"Then know what you mean."

SEPTEMBER 5

THE PRINCESS CASAMASSIMA, 1886

For this unfortunate but remarkably organized youth every displeasure or gratification of the visual sense coloured his whole mind, and though he lived in Pentonville and worked in Soho, though he was poor and obscure and cramped and full of unattainable desires, it may be said of him that what was most important in life for him was simply his impressions. They came from everything he touched, they kept him thrilling and throbbing through considerable parts of his waking consciousness, and they constituted as yet the principal events and stages of his career. Fortunately they were sometimes very delightful. Everything in the field of observation suggested this or that; everything struck him, penetrated, stirred; he had, in a word, more impressions than he knew what to do with—felt sometimes as if they would consume or asphyxiate him.

SEPTEMBER 6

THE AMBASSADORS, 1903

These were instants at which he could ask whether, since there had been, fundamentally, so little question of his keeping anything, the fate after all decreed for him hadn't been only to *be* kept. Kept for something, in that event, that he didn't pretend, didn't possibly dare, as yet, to divine; something that made him hover and wonder and laugh and sigh, made him advance and retreat, feeling half ashamed of his impulse to plunge and more than half afraid of his impulse to wait.

SEPTEMBER 7

WHAT MAISIE KNEW, 1898

Maisie could appreciate her fatigue; the day hadn't passed without such an observer's discovering that she was excited and even mentally comparing her state to that of the breakers after a gale.

SEPTEMBER 8

THE PAPERS, 1903

"I want, while I'm about it, to pity him in sufficient quantity."
"Precisely, which means, for a woman, with extravagance and to the point of immorality."

SEPTEMBER 9

JAMES RUSSELL LOWELL, 1891

His robust and humourous optimism rounds itself more and more; he has even now something of the air of a classic, and if he really becomes one it will be in virtue of his having placed as fine an irony at the service of hope as certain masters of the other strain have placed at that of despair.

SEPTEMBER 10

RODERICK HUDSON, 1875

He had felt an angry desire to protest against a destiny which seemed determined to be exclusively salutary. It seemed to him he should bear a little spoiling.

SEPTEMBER 11

RODERICK HUDSON, 1875

The moods of an artist, his exultations and depressions, Rowland had often said to himself, were like the pen flourishes a writing master makes in the air when he begins to set his copy. He may bespatter you with ink, he may hit you in the eye, but he writes a magnificent hand.

SEPTEMBER 12

THE AMBASSADOR, 1903

The fact that he had failed, as he considered in everything, in each relation and in half a dozen trades, as he liked luxuriously to put it, might have made, might still make for an empty present, but stood expressively for a crowded past. It had not been, so much achievement missed, a light yoke nor a short road. It was at present as if the backward picture had hung there, the long crooked course, gray in the shadow of his solitude. It had been a dreadful, cheerful, sociable solitude, a solitude of life, of choice, of community; but though there had been people enough all round it, there had been but three or four persons in it.

SEPTEMBER 13

THE LETTERS OF ROBERT LOUIS STEVENSON, 1900

Fate, as if to distinguish him as handsomely as possible, seemed to be ever treating him to some chance for an act or a course that had almost nothing in its favor but its inordinate difficulty. If the difficulty was, in these cases, not *all* the beauty for him, it at least never prevented his finding in it— or our finding, at any rate, as observers—so much beauty as comes from a great risk accepted either for an idea or for simple joy.

SEPTEMBER 14

THE PRINCESS CASAMASSIMA, 1886

"At any rate he would have conformed to the great religious rule—to live each hour as if it were to be one's last."

"In holiness you mean—in great *receuillement*?" the Princess asked.

"Oh dear, no; simply in extreme thankfulness for every minute that's added."

SEPTEMBER 15

THE LESSON OF THE MASTER, 1892

"Ah, perfection, perfection—how one ought to go in for it! I wish I could."

"Everyone can in his way," said Paul Overt.

"In *his* way, yes; but not in hers. Women are so hampered—so condemned! But it's a kind of dishonour if you don't, when you want to *do* something, isn't it?"

SEPTEMBER 16

THE GOLDEN BOWL, 1904

The extent to which they enjoyed their indifference to any judgment of their want of ceremony, what did that of itself speak but for the way, that, as a rule, they almost equally had others on their mind? They each knew that both were full of the superstition of "not hurting," but might precisely have been asking themselves, asking in fact each other, at this moment, whether that was to be, after all, the last word of their conscientious development.

SEPTEMBER 17

THE PORTRAIT OF A LADY, 1881

"What is *your* idea of success?"

"You evidently think it must be very tame," said Isabel.

"It's to see some dream of one's youth come true."

SEPTEMBER 18

THE ART OF FICTION, 1884

Discussion, suggestion, formulation, these things are fertilizing when they are frank and sincere.

SEPTEMBER 19

THE PRINCESS CASAMASSIMA, 1886

He saw the immeasurable misery of the people, and yet he saw all that had been, as it were, rescued and redeemed from it: the treasures, the felicities, the splendours, the successes of the world.

SEPTEMBER 20

Rowland complimented her on her fund of useful information.

"It's not especially useful," she answered; "but I like to know the names of plants as I do those of my acquaintances. When we walk in the woods at home—which we do so much—it seems as unnatural not to know what to call the flowers as it would be to see some one in the town with whom we should not be on speaking terms."

SEPTEMBER 21

There, in its place, *was* life—with all its rage; the vague unrest of the need for action knew it again, the stir of the faculty that had been refreshed and reconsecrated.

SEPTEMBER 22

Anyhow, he went forth again into the streets, into the squares, into the parks, solicited by an aimless desire to steep himself yet once again in the great indifferent city which he knew and loved and which had had so many of his smiles and tears and confidences.

SEPTEMBER 23

THE GOLDEN BOWL, 1904

There was something in Adam Verver's eyes that both admitted the morning and the evening in unusual quantities and gave the modest area the outward extension of a view that was "big" even when restricted to the stars. Deeply and changeably blue, though not romantically large, they were yet youthfully, almost strangely beautiful, with their ambiguity of your scarce knowing if they most carried their possessor's vision out or most opened themselves to your own.

SEPTEMBER 24

THE WINGS OF THE DOVE, 1903

Her welcome, her frankness, sweetness, sadness, brightness, her disconcerting poetry, as he made shift at moments to call it, helped as it was by the beauty of her whole setting and by the perception, at the same time, on the observer's part, that this element gained from her, in a manner, for effect and harmony, as much as it gave—her whole attitude had, to his imagination, meanings that hung about

it, waiting upon her, hovering, dropping and qua-
vering forth again, like vague, faint, snatches, mere
ghosts of sound, of old-fashioned melancholy music.

SEPTEMBER 25

THE OTHER HOUSE, 1896

It would do with the question what it was Mrs. Beev-
er's inveterate household practice to do with all
loose and unarranged objects—it would get it out
of the way. There would have been difficulty in say-
ing whether it was a I feeling for peace or for war, but
her constant habit was to I lay the ground bare for
complications that as yet at least had never taken
place. Her life was like a room prepared for a dance:
the furniture was all against the walls.

SEPTEMBER 26

THE PRINCESS CASAMASSIMA, 1886

"I haven't the least objection to his feeling badly;
that's not the worst thing in the world! If a few more
people felt badly, in this sodden, stolid, stupid race
of ours, the world would wake up to an idea or two,
and we should see the beginning of the dance. It's
the dull acceptance, the absence of reflection, the
impenetrable density."

SEPTEMBER 27

The great historic house had—beyond terrace and garden, as the centre of an almost extravagantly grand Watteau composition, a tone as of old gold kept "down" by the quality of the air, summer full-flushed, but attuned to the general perfect taste.

SEPTEMBER 28

"Her head has great character, great natural style. If a woman is not to be a brilliant beauty in the regular way, she will choose, if she's wise, to look like that. She will not be thought pretty by people in general, and desecrated, as she passes, by the stare of every vile wretch who chooses to thrust his nose under her bonnet; but a certain number of intelligent people will find it one of the delightful things of life to look at her. That lot is as good as another! Then she has a beautiful character."

SEPTEMBER 29

"I sometimes ask myself if it's quite fair. Fair I mean to have so involved and—since we may say it—interested you. I almost feel as if you hadn't really had time to do anything else."

"Anything else but be interested?" she asked. "Ah, what else does one ever want to be?"

SEPTEMBER 30

She gave an envious thought to the happier lot of men, who are always free to plunge into the healing waters of action.

OCTOBER

It might be an ado about trifles—and half the poetry, roundabout, the poetry in solution in the air, was doubtless but the alertness of the touch of Autumn, the imprisoned painter, the Bohemian with a rusty jacket, who had already broken out with palette and brush; yet the way the color begins in those days to be dabbed, the way, here and there, for a start, a solitary maple on a woodside flames in single scarlet, recalls nothing so much as the daughter of a noble house dressed for a fancy-ball, with the whole family gathered round to admire her before she goes. One speaks, at the same time of the orchards; but there are properly no orchards when half the countryside shows, the easiest, most familiar sacrifice to Pomona. The apple tree in New England plays the part of the olive in Italy, charges itself with the effect of detail, for the most part otherwise too scantly produced, and, engaged in this charming care, becomes infinitely decorative and delicate. What it must do for the too under-dressed land in May and June is easily supposable; but its office in the early autumn is to scatter coral and gold. The apples are everywhere and every interval, every old clearing, an orchard. You pick them up from under your feet but to bite into them, for fellowship, and throw them away; but as you catch their young brightness in the blue air, where they suggest strings of strange-colored pearls tangled in the knotted boughs, as you notice their manner of swarming for a brief and wasted gayety, they seem to ask to be praised only by the cheerful shepherd and the oaten pipe.

New England: An Autumn Impression, 1905

OCTOBER 1

"What I hate is myself—when I think that one has to take so much, to be happy, out of the lives of others, and that one isn't happy, even then. One does it to cheat one's self and to stop one's mouth—but that's only, at the best, for a little. The wretched self is always there, always making one somehow a fresh anxiety. What it comes to is this, that it's not, that it's never, a happiness, any happiness at all, to *take*. The only safe thing is to give. It's what plays you least false."

OCTOBER 2

"He did his best at a venture." I went in and turned my steps to the chapel of the tombs. Viewing in sadness the sadness of its immortal treasures, I fancied, while I stood there, that they needed no ampler commentary than those simple words.

OCTOBER 3

A MOST EXTRAORDINARY CASE, 1868

For ten long days, the most memorable days of his life—days which, if he had kept a journal, would have been left blank—he held his tongue.

OCTOBER 4

THE GOLDEN BOWL, 1904

She had found sympathy her best resource. It gave her plenty to do; it made her, as she also said, sit up. She had in her life two great holes to fill, and she described herself as dropping social scraps into them as she had known old ladies, in her early American time, drop morsels of silk into the baskets in which they collected the material for some eventual patchwork quilt.

OCTOBER 5

THE PORTRAIT OF A LADY, 1881

You think that you can lead a romantic life, that you can live by pleasing yourself and pleasing others. You'll find you are mistaken. Whatever life you lead you must put your soul into it—to make any sort of success of it; and from the moment you do that it ceases to be romance, I assure you; it becomes reality! And you can't always please yourself; you must sometimes please other people. That, I admit, you are very ready to do; but there is another thing that is still more important—you must often *dis*please others. You must always be ready for that—you must never shrink from it."

OCTOBER 6

THE PORTRAIT OF A LADY, 1881

"I like places in which things have happened—even if they are sad things."

OCTOBER 7

THE WINGS OF THE DOVE, 1903

The weather changed, the stubborn storm yielded, and the autumn sunshine, baffled for many days, but now hot and almost vindictive, came into its own again and, with an almost audible paean, a suffusion of bright sound that was one with the bright colour, took large possession. Venice glowed and plashed and called and chimed again; the air was like a clap of hands, and the scattered pinks, yellows, blues, sea-greens, were like a hanging-out of vivid stuffs, a laying down of fine carpets.

OCTOBER 8

"What it comes to is the way she believes in one. That is if she believes at all."

"Yes that's what it comes to."

"And why should it be terrible?"

"Because it's always so—the idea of having to pity people."

"Not when there's also the idea of helping them."

"Yes, but if we can't help them?"

"We *can*—we always can. That is," he competently added, "if we care for them."

OCTOBER 9

"A man with as good a head and heart as yours has a very ample world within himself, and I'm no believer in art for art, nor in what's called 'life for life's sake.' Nevertheless take your plunge, and come and tell me whether you've found the pearl of wisdom."

OCTOBER 10

"I believe enough things about you, my dear, to have a few left if most of them, even, go to smash. I've taken care of *that*. I've divided my faith into water-tight compartments. We must manage not to sink."

"You do believe I'm not a hypocrite? You recognize that I don't lie or dissemble or deceive? Is *that* water-tight?"

"Water-tight—the biggest compartment of all? Why, it's the best cabin and the main deck and the engine-room and the steward's pantry! It's the ship itself—it's the whole line. It's the captain's table and all one's luggage—one's reading for the trip."

OCTOBER 11

"My idea is this, that when you only love a little you're naturally not jealous—or are only jealous also a little, so that it doesn't matter. But when you love in a deeper and intenser way, then you are, in the same proportion, jealous; your jealousy has intensity and, no doubt, ferocity. When, however, you love in the most abysmal and unutterable way of all—why then you're beyond everything, and nothing can pull you down."

OCTOBER 12

THE PAPERS, 1903

She knew little enough of what she might have to do for him, but her hope, as sharp as a pang, was that, if anything, it would put her in danger too.

OCTOBER 13

THE WINGS OF THE DOVE, 1903

Certainly it came from the sweet taste of solitude, caught again and cherished for the hour; always a need of her nature, moreover, when things spoke to her with penetration. It was mostly in stillness that they spoke to her best; amid voices she lost the sense.

OCTOBER 14

THE BOSTONIANS, 1886

Positive it is that she spared herself none of the inductions of a reverie that seemed to dry up the mists and ambiguities of life. These hours of back-ward clearness come to all men and women, once at least, when they read the past in the light of the present, with the reasons of things, like unobserved finger-posts, protruding where they never saw them before. The journey behind them is mapped out and figured, with its false steps, its wrong observations, all its infatuated, deluded geography.

OCTOBER 15

THE PORTRAIT OF A LADY, 1881

To be so graceful, so gracious, so wise, so good, and to make so light of it all—that was really to be a great lady.

OCTOBER 16

THE PRINCESS CASAMASSIMA, 1886

"I'm acquainted with many of our most important men."
"Do you mention it as a guarantee, so that I may know you're genuine?"
"Not exactly; that would be weak, wouldn't it?" the Princess asked. "My genuineness must be in myself—a matter for you to appreciate as you know me better; not in my references and vouchers."

OCTOBER 17

"I suppose we are a genus by ourselves in the providential scheme—we talents that can't act, that can't do not dare. We take it out in talk, in plans and promises, in study, in visions. But our visions, let me tell you—have a way of being brilliant, and a man has not lived in vain who has seen the things I've seen!"

OCTOBER 18

"Great in nature, in character, in spirit. Great in life."
"So?" Mr. Verver echoed, "What has she done—in life?"
"Well she has been brave and bright," said Maggie.
"That mayn't sound like much, but she has been so in the face of things that might well have made it too difficult for many other girls."

OCTOBER 19

But half the satisfaction of the spot, for this mysterious and fitful worshipper, was that he found the years of his life there, and the ties, the affections, the struggles, the submissions, the conquests—all conducing as to a record of that adventurous journey in which the beginnings and the endings of human relations are the lettered mile-stones.

OCTOBER 20

RODERICK HUDSON, 1875

The vivacity of his perceptions, the audacity of his imagination, the picturesqueness of his phrase when he was pleased—and even more when he was displeased—his abounding good-humour, his candour, his unclouded frankness, his unfailing impulse to share every emotion and impression with his friend; all this made comradeship a high felicity.

OCTOBER 21

FRENCH POETS AND NOVELISTS, 1878

The personal optimism of most of us no romancer can confirm or dissipate, and our personal troubles, generally, place fiction of all kinds in an impertinent light.

OCTOBER 22

It came to him in fact that just here was his usual case: he was forever missing things through his general genius for missing them, while others were forever picking them up through a contrary bent. And it was others who looked abstemious and he who looked greedy; it was he, somehow, who finally paid, and it was others who mainly partook. Yes, he should go to the scaffold yet for he wouldn't quite know whom.

OCTOBER 23

The talk was so low, with pauses somehow so not of embarrassment that it could only have been earnest, and the air, an air of privilege and privacy to our young woman's sense, seemed charged with fine things taken for granted.

OCTOBER 24

One of the things she loved him for, however, was that he gave you touching surprises in this line, had sudden inconsistencies of temper that were all to your advantage. He was by no means always mild when he ought to have been, but he was sometimes so when there was no obligation.

OCTOBER 25

IVAN TURGÉNIEFF, 1878

Sanin's history is weighted with the moral that salvation lies in being able, at a given moment, to turn on one's will like a screw. If Mr. Turgénieff pays his tribute to the magic of sense he leaves us also eloquently reminded that soul in the long run claims her own.

OCTOBER 26

THE REVERBERATOR, 1888

The old gentleman, heaven knew, had prejudices, but if they were numerous, and some of them very curious, they were not rigid. He had also such nice inconsistent feelings, such irrepressible indulgences, and they would ease everything off.

Surprise, it was true, was not, on the other hand, what the eyes of Strether's friend most showed him. They had taken hold of him straightway, measuring him up and down, as if they knew how; as if he were human material they had already in some sort handled. Their possessor was in truth, it may be communicated, the mistress of a hundred cases or categories, receptacles of the mind, subdivisions for convenience, in which, from a full experience, she pigeon-holed her fellow-mortals with a hand as free as that of a compositor scattering type.

OCTOBER 28

WHAT MAISIE KNEW, 1898

"If you'll help me, you know, I'll help *you*," he concluded in the pleasant fraternizing, equalizing, not a bit patronizing way which made the child ready to go through anything for him, and the beauty of which, as she dimly felt, was that it was not a deceitful descent to her years, but a real indifference to them.

OCTOBER 29

THE AWKWARD AGE, 1899

A suppositious spectator would certainly, on this, have imagined in the girl's face the delicate dawn of a sense that her mother had suddenly become vulgar, together with a general consciousness that the way to meet vulgarity was always to be frank and simple.

OCTOBER 30

THE NEXT TIME, 1895

The only success worth one's powder was success in the line of one's idiosyncrasy. Consistency was in itself distinction, and what was talent but the art of being completely whatever it was that one happened to be? One's things were characteristic or were nothing.

OCTOBER 31

THE PORTRAIT OF A LADY, 1881

She often checked herself with the thought of the thousands of people who were less happy than herself—a thought which for the moment made her absorbing happiness appear to her a kind of immodesty. What should we do with the misery of the world in a scheme of the agreeable for oneself?

NOVEMBER

I think the romance of a winter afternoon in London arises partly from the fact that when it is not altogether smothered the general lamp-light takes this hue of hospitality. Such is the colour of the interior glow of the clubs in Pall Mall, which I positively like best when the fog loiters upon their monumental stair-cases. . . . London is infinite. It is one of your pleasures to think of the experiments and excursions you may make in it, even when the adventures don't particularly come off. The friendly fog seems to protect and enrich them—to add both to the mystery and security, so that it is most in the winter months that the imagination weaves such delights.—Then the big fires blaze in the lone twilight of the clubs, and the new books on the tables say, "now at last you have time to read me," and the afternoon tea and toast appear to make the assurance good. It is not a small matter either, to a man of letters, that this is the best time for writing, and that during the lamp-lit days the white page he tries to blacken becomes, on his table, in the circle of the lamp, with the screen of the climate folding him in, more vivid and absorbent. The weather makes a kind of sedentary midnight and muffles the possible interruptions. It's bad for the eyesight, but excellent for the image.

Essays in London and Elsewhere, 1893

༺ ༄

NOVEMBER 1

RODERICK HUDSON, 1875

"A man should make the most of himself and be helped if he needs help," Rowland answered after a long pause. "Of course when a body begins to expand, there comes in the possibility of bursting; but I nevertheless approve of a certain tension of one's being. It's what a man is meant for. And then I believe in the essential salubrity of genius—true genius."

NOVEMBER 2

THE BOSTONIANS, 1886

Miss Birdseye had given herself away so lavishly all her life that it was rather odd there was anything left of her for the supreme surrender.

NOVEMBER 3

THE PRINCESS CASAMASSIMA, 1886

Hyacinth had roamed through the great city since he was an urchin, but his imagination had never ceased to be stirred by the preparations for Sunday that went on in the evening among the toilers and spinners, his brothers and sisters, and he lost himself in all the quickened crowding and pushing and staring at lighted windows and chaffering at the stalls of fishmongers and hucksters. He liked the people who looked as if they had got their week's wage and were prepared to lay it out discreetly; and even those whose use of it would plainly be extravagant and intemperate; and best of all, those who evidently hadn't received it at all and who wandered about, disinterestedly, vaguely, with their hands in empty pockets, watching others make their bargains and fill their satchels, or staring at the striated sides of bacon, at the golden cubes and triangles of cheese, at the graceful festoons of sausage, in the most brilliant windows.

NOVEMBER 4

RODERICK HUDSON, 1875

His was neither an irresponsibly contemplative nature nor a sturdily practical one, and he was forever looking in vain for the uses of the things that please and the charm of the things that sustain. He was an awkward mixture of moral and aesthetic curiosity, and yet he would have made an ineffective reformer and an indifferent artist. It seemed to him that the glow of happiness must be found either in action of some immensely solid kind on behalf of an idea, or in producing a masterpiece in one of the arts.

NOVEMBER 5

BROKEN WINGS, 1903

One had but one's hour, and if one had it soon—it was really almost a case of choice—one didn't have it late.

NOVEMBER 6

THE PUPIL, 1892

The Moreens were adventurers not merely because they didn't pay their debts, because they lived on society, but because their whole view of life, dim and confused and instinctive, like that of clever colour-blind animals, was speculative and rapacious and mean—they were adventurers because they were abject snobs.

NOVEMBER 7

THE EUROPEANS, 1878

Never was a nature more perfectly fortunate. It was not a restless, apprehensive, ambitious spirit, running a race with the tyranny of fate, but a temper so unsuspicious as to put adversity off her guard, dodging and evading her with the easy, natural motion of a wind-shifted flower.

NOVEMBER 8

THE PUPIL, 1892

They had a theory that they were very thorough, and yet they seemed always to be in the amusing part of lessons, the intervals between the tunnels, where there were way sides and views.

NOVEMBER 9

RODERICK HUDSON, 1875

Surely youth and genius hand in hand were the most beautiful sight in the world.

NOVEMBER 10

THE WINGS OF THE DOVE, 1903

The beauty of the bloom had gone from the small old sense of safety—that was distinct. She had left it behind her there forever. But the beauty of the idea of a great adventure, a big dim experiment or struggle in which she might, more responsibly than ever before, take a hand, had been offered her instead. It was as if she had to pluck off her breast, to throw away, some friendly ornament, a familiar flower, a little old jewel, that was part of her daily dress, and to take up and shoulder as a substitute some queer defensive weapon, a musket, a spear, a battleaxe—conducive possibly in a higher degree to a striking appearance, but demanding all the effort of the military posture.

NOVEMBER 11

THE LESSON OF THE MASTER, 1892

"Look at me well and take my lesson to heart, for it is a lesson. Let that good come of it at least that you shudder with your pitiful impression and that this may help to keep you straight in the future. Don't become in your old age what I am in mine—the depressing, the deplorable illustration of the worship of false gods!"

"What do you mean by false gods?" Paul inquired.

"The idols of the market—money and luxury and 'the world,' placing one's children and dressing one's wife—everything that drives one to the short and easy way. Ah, the vile things they make one do!"

NOVEMBER 12

THE AMBASSADORS, 1903

Only a few of Chad's guests had dined—that is fifteen or twenty, a few compared with the large concourse offered to sight by eleven o'clock; but number and mass, quantity and quality, light, fragrance, sound, the overflow of hospitality meeting the high tide of response, had all, from the first, pressed upon Strether's consciousness, and he felt himself somehow part and parcel of the most festive scene, as the term was, in which he had ever in his life been engaged.

NOVEMBER 13

THE LETTERS OF ROBERT LOUIS STEVENSON, 1900

The fascination in him from the first is the mixture, and the extraordinary charm of his letters is that they are always showing this. It is the proportions, moreover, that are so admirable—the quantity of each different thing that he fitted to each other one and to the whole. The free life would have been all his dream, if so large a part of it had not been that love of letters, of expression and form, which is but another name for the life of service. Almost the last word about him, by the same law, would be that he had, at any rate, supremely written, were it not that he seems still better characterized by his having at any rate supremely lived.

[ROBERT LOUIS STEVENSON BORN ON THIS DAY IN 1850]

NOVEMBER 14

THE GOLDEN BOWL, 1904

"I wouldn't in any case have let her tell me what would have been dreadful to me—I don't *want* to know! There are things that are sacred—whether they're joys or pains. But one can always, for safety, be kind," she kept on; "one feels when that's right."

NOVEMBER 15

THE PRINCESS CASAMASSIMA, 1886

"She always looks the same: like an angel who came down from heaven yesterday and has been rather disappointed in her first day on earth."

NOVEMBER 16

THE LESSON OF THE MASTER, 1892

"What I mean is, have you it in your mind to go in for some sort of little perfection? You must have thought it all over, I can't believe you're without a plan. That's the sensation you give me, and it's so rare that it really stirs up one; it makes you remarkable."

NOVEMBER 17

Most forms of contempt are unwise; but one of them seems to us peculiarly ridiculous—contempt for the age one lives in. Men with but a little of Mérimée's ingenuity have been able, and have not failed, in every age, to make out a deplorable case for mankind. His imagination faded early, and it is certainly a question whether this generous spirit, half-sister at least to charity, will remain under a roof in which the ideal is treated as uncivilly as Mérimée treated it.

NOVEMBER 18

THE WINGS OF THE DOVE, 1903

Whatever were the facts, their perfect manners, all round, saw them through.

NOVEMBER 19

THE WINGS OF THE DOVE, 1903

Mrs. Stringham's little life had often been visited by shy conceits—secret dreams that had fluttered their hour between its narrow walls, without, for any great part; so much as mustering courage to look out of its rather dim windows.

NOVEMBER 20

THE PORTRAIT OF A LADY, 1881

"Take things more easily. Don't ask so much whether this or that is good for you. Don't question your conscience so much—it will get out of tune, like a strummed piano. Keep it for great occasions. Don't try so much to form your character—it's like trying to pull open a rose-bud."

NOVEMBER 21

THE PAPERS, 1903

Their general irony, which they tried at the same time to keep gay and to make amusing at least to each other, was their refuge from the want of savour, the want of napkins, the want, too often of shillings, and of many things besides that they would have liked to have.

NOVEMBER 22

THE LIFE OF GEORGE ELIOT, 1885

George Eliot of course had drawbacks and difficulties, physical infirmities, constant liabilities to headache, dyspepsia, and other illness, to deep depression, to despair about her work; but these jolts of the chariot were small in proportion to the impetus acquired, and were hardly greater than was necessary for reminding her of the secret of all ambitious workers in the field of art—that effort, effort, always effort, is the only key to success. Her great furtherance was that, intensely intellectual being as she was, the life of affection and emotion was also widely open to her.

[GEORGE ELIOT BORN ON THIS DAY IN 1819]

NOVEMBER 23
THE AWKWARD AGE, 1899

"Will she understand? She has everything in the world but one," he added. "But that's half."
"What is it?"
"A sense of humor."

NOVEMBER 24
LOUISE PALLANT, 1888

Never say you know the last word about any human heart! I was once treated to a revelation which startled and touched me, in the nature of a person with whom I had been acquainted (well, as I supposed) for years, whose character I had had good reasons, heaven knows, to appreciate and in regard to whom I flattered myself that I had nothing more to learn.

NOVEMBER 25

"I'm a little mad, you know; you needn't be surprised if you hear it. That's because I stop in town when they go into the country; all the autumn, all the winter, when there's no one here (save three or four millions), and the rain drips, drips, drips from the trees in the big dull park where my people live."

NOVEMBER 26

He suggested above all, however, that wondrous state of youth in which the elements, the metals more or less precious, are so in fusion and fermentation that the question of the final stamp, the pressure that fixes the value, must wait for comparative coolness.

NOVEMBER 27

I remember that at the play she often said, "Yes, they're funny; but they don't begin to know how funny they might be!" Mrs. Kemble always knew, and her good humor effectually forearmed her. She had more "habits" than most people have room in life for, and a theory that to a person of her disposition they were as necessary as the close meshes of a strait-waistcoat. If she had not lived by rule (on her showing), she would have lived infallibly by riot. Her rules and her riots, her reservations and her concessions, all her luxuriant theory and all her extravagant practice, her drollery that mocked at her melancholy, her imagination that mocked at her drollery, and her rare forms and personal traditions that mocked a little at everything—these were part of the constant freshness which made those who loved her love her so much.

[FANNY KEMBLE BORN ON THIS DAY IN 1809]

NOVEMBER 28

THE PORTRAIT OF A LADY, 1881

"We know too much about people in these days; we hear too much. Our ears, our minds, our mouths, are stuffed with personalities. Don't mind anything that anyone tells you about anyone else. Judge everyone and everything for yourself."

NOVEMBER 29
THE NEXT TIME, 1895

The happiness that sat with us when we talked and that made it always amusing to talk, the sense of his being on the heels of success, coming closer and closer, touching it at last, knowing that he should touch it again and hold it fast and hold it high.

NOVEMBER 30
THE WINGS OF THE DOVE, 1903

"The very essence of her, as you surely by this time have made out for yourself, is that, when she adopts a view, she—well to her own sense, really brings the thing about, fairly terrorizes with her view any other, an opposite view, and those with it who represent it."

DECEMBER

There was a splendid sky, all blue-black and silver—
a sparkling wintry vault where the stars were like a
myriad points of ice. The air was silent and sharp,
and the vague snow looked cruel.

The Bostonians, 1886

———

The early dusk had gathered thick, but the evening
was fine and the lighted streets had the animation
and variety of a winter that had begun with brilliancy. The shop fronts glowed through frosty panes,
the bells of the street cars jangled in the cold air,
the newsboys hawked the evening-paper, the vesti-
bules of the theatres, illuminated and flanked with
colored posters and the photographs of actresses,
exhibited seductively their swinging doors of red
leather or baize, spotted with little brass nails. Behind great plates of glass the interior of the hotels
became visible, with marble-paved lobbies, white
with electric lamps, and columns, and Westerners
on divans stretching their legs, while behind a coun-
ter, set apart and covered with an array of periodi-

cals and novels in paper covers, little boys, with the faces of old men, showing plans of the play houses and offering librettos, sold orchestra chairs at a premium.

The Bostonians, 1886

ᴄ❦ᴐ

DECEMBER 1

RODERICK HUDSON, 1875

He felt the fiction of existence more than was sus-
pected; but he asked no allowance on grounds of
temper, he assumed that fate had treated him inor-
dinately well and that he had no excuse for taking an
ill-natured view of life, and he undertook to believe
that all women were fair, all men were brave, and
the world was a delightful place of sojourn, until the
contrary should be distinctly proved.

DECEMBER 2

THE GOLDEN BOWL, 1904

Variety of imagination—what is that but fatal, in the
world of affairs, unless so disciplined as not to be
distinguished from monotony?

DECEMBER 3

THE LETTERS OF ROBERT LOUIS STEVENSON, 1900

Stevenson never covered his tracks, and the tracks
prove perhaps to be what most attaches us. We follow them here from year to year and from stage to
stage, with the same charmed sense with which he
has made us follow one of his hunted herds in the

heather. Life and fate and an early catastrophe were ever at his heels, and when he at last falls fighting, sinks down in the very act of valor, the "happy ending," as he calls it for some of his correspondents, is, though precipitated and not conventional, assuredly there.

DECEMBER 4

THE LETTERS OF ROBERT LOUIS STEVENSON, 1900

It took his own delightful talk to show how more than absurd it might be, and, if convenient, how very obscurely so, that such an incurable rover should have been complicated both with such an incurable scribbler and sad and incurable invalid, and that a man should find himself such an anomaly as a drenched yachtsman haunted with "style," a shameless Bohemian haunted with duty, and a victim at once of the personal hunger and instinct for adventure and of the critical, constructive, sedentary view of it. He had everything all round— adventure most of all; to feel which we have only to turn from the beautiful flush of it in his text to the scarce less beautiful vision of the great hilltop in Pacific seas to which, after death, he was borne by islanders and chiefs.

"You women are all the same! But the type to which your brother belongs was made to be the ruin of you, and you were made to be its handmaids and victims. The sign of the type in question is the determination—sometimes terrible in its quiet intensity—to accept nothing of life but its pleasures, and secure the pleasures chiefly by the aid of your complaisant sex. Young men of this class never do anything for themselves that they can get other people to do for them, and it is the infatuation, the devotion, the superstition of others, that keeps them going. These others in ninety-nine cases out of a hundred are women. What our young friends chiefly insist upon is that someone else shall suffer for them; and women do that sort of thing, as you must know, wonderfully well."

DECEMBER 6

THE AWKWARD AGE, 1899

It was a mark of the special intercourse of these good friends that though they had for each other, in manner and tone, such a fund of consideration as might almost have given it the stamp of diplomacy, there was yet in it also something of that economy

of expression which is the result of a common experience.

DECEMBER 7

THE WINGS OF THE DOVE, 1903

She was a success, that was what it came to and that
was what it was to be a success: it always happened
before one could know it. One's ignorance was in
fact often the greatest part of it.

DECEMBER 8

THE GREAT CONDITION, 1900

"There it practically was, this experience, in the
character of her delicacy, in her kindly, witty, sensi-
tive face, worn fine, too fine perhaps, but only to
its increase of expression. She was neither a young
fool nor an old one, assuredly; but if the intenser
acquaintance with life had made the object of one's
affection neither false nor hard, how could one, on
the whole, since the story might be so interesting,
wish it away?"

DECEMBER 9

Hyacinth found it less amusing, but the theatre, in any conditions, was full of sweet deception for him. His imagination projected, itself lovingly across the footlights, gilded and coloured the shabby canvas and battered accessories, and lost itself so effectually in the future world that the end of the piece, however long, or however short, brought with it a kind of alarm, like a stoppage of his personal life. It was impossible to be more friendly to the dramatic illusion.

DECEMBER 10

His duty was obscure, but he never lost a certain private satisfaction in remembering that on two or three occasions it had been performed with something of an ideal precision.

DECEMBER 11

It had ever been her sign that she was, for all occasions, *found* ready, without loose ends or exposed accessories or unremoved superfluities; a suggestion of the swept and garnished, in her whole splendid, yet thereby more or less encumbered and embroidered setting, that reflected her small still passion for order and symmetry, for objects with their backs to the walls, and spoke even of some probable reference, in her American blood, to dusting and polishing New England grandmothers.

DECEMBER 12

THE LESSON OF THE MASTER, 1892

The quiet face had a charm which increased in proportion as it became completely quiet. The change to the expression of gaiety excited on Overt's part a private protest which resembled that of a person sitting in the twilight and enjoying it, when the lamp is brought in too soon.

DECEMBER 13

A LANDSCAPE PAINTER, 1866

"To be young, strong and poor—such in this blessed nineteenth century, is the great basis of solid success."

DECEMBER 14

The tokens of a chastened ease, after all, still abounded, many marks of a taste whose discriminations might perhaps have been called eccentric. He guessed at intense little preferences and sharp little exclusions, a deep suspicion of the vulgar and a personal view of the right. The general result of this was something for which he had no name, on the spot, quite ready, but something he would have come nearest to naming in speaking of it as the air of supreme respectability, the consciousness, small, still, reserved, but none the less distinct and diffused, of private honor.

DECEMBER 15

He had passed his life in estimating people (it was part of the medical trade), and in nineteen cases out of twenty he was right.

DECEMBER 16

So ordered and so splendid a rest, all the tokens, spreading about them, of confidence solidly supported, might have suggested for persons of poorer pitch the very insolence of facility. Still, they weren't insolent—they weren't—they were only blissful and grateful and personally modest, not ashamed of knowing, with competence, when great things were great, when good things were good, and when safe things were safe, and not, therefore, placed below their fortune by timidity; which would have been as bad as being below it by impudence.

DECEMBER 17

"For how *can*, how need a woman be 'proud' who's so preternaturally clever? Pride's only for use when wit breaks down—it's the train the cyclist takes when his tire's deflated."

DECEMBER 18

He was struck with the tack, the taste of her vagueness, which simply took for granted in him a sense of beautiful things. He was conscious of how much it was affected, this sense, by something subdued and discreet in the way she had arranged herself for her special object and her morning walk—he believed her to have come on foot; the way her slightly thicker veil was drawn—a mere touch, but everything; the composed gravity of her dress, in which here and there, a dull wine-color seemed to gleam faintly through black; the charming discretion of her small, compact head; the quiet note, as she sat, of her folded, gray-gloved hands.

DECEMBER 19

RODERICK HUDSON, 1875

"Upon my word I'm not happy! I'm clever enough to want more than I have got. I'm tired of myself, my own thoughts, my own affairs, my own eternal company. True happiness, we are told, consists in getting out of one's self, but the point is not only to get out—you must stay out; and to stay out you must have some absorbing errand."

DECEMBER 20

THE AMBASSADORS, 1903

"Is Mamie a great *parti*?"

"Oh, the greatest we have—our prettiest, brightest girl."

"I know what they *can* be. And with money?"

"Not perhaps a great deal of that—but with so much of everything else that we don't miss it. We *don't* miss money much, you know," Strether added, "in general, in America, in pretty girls."

DECEMBER 21

THE NEXT TIME, 1895

I would cross the scent with something showily impossible, splendidly unpopular.

DECEMBER 22

THE AMBASSADORS, 1903

Above all she suggested to him the reflection that the *femme du monde*—in these finest developments of the type—was, like Cleopatra in the play, indeed various and multifold. She had aspects, characters, days, nights—or had them at least, showed them by a mysterious law of her own, when in addition to everything she happened also to be a woman of genius. She was an obscure person, a muffled person one day; and a showy person, an uncovered person, the next.

DECEMBER 23

THE GOLDEN BOWL, 1904

Such connection as he enjoyed with the ironic question in general resided substantially less in a personal use of it than in the habit of seeing it as easy to others. He was so framed by nature as to be able to keep his inconveniences separate from his resentments.

DECEMBER 24

THE WINGS OF THE DOVE, 1903

They were on the edge of Christmas, but Christmas, this year was, as, in London, in so many other years, disconcertingly mild; the still air was soft, the thick light was grey, the great town looked empty, and in the Park, where the grass was green, where the sheep browsed, where the birds multitudinously twittered, the straight walks lent themselves to slowness and the dim vistas to privacy.

DECEMBER 25

No shrine could be more decked and no ceremonial more stately than those to which his worship was attached. He had no imagination about these things save that they were accessible to every one who should ever feel the need of them. The poorest could build such temples of the spirit—could make them blaze with candles and smoke with incense, make them flush with pictures and flowers. The cost, in common phrase, of keeping them up fell entirely on the liberal heart.

DECEMBER 26

WHAT MAISIE KNEW, 1898

She was at the age when all stories are true and all conceptions are stories. The actual was the absolute; the present alone was vivid.

DECEMBER 27

THE WINGS OF THE DOVE, 1903

It was an oddity of Mrs. Lowder's that her face in speech was like a lighted window at night, but that silence immediately drew the curtain.

DECEMBER 28

They were above all in that phase of youth and in that I state of aspiration in which "luck" is the subject of most I frequent recurrence, as definite as the colour red, and in which it is the elegant name for money when people are is refined as they are poor.

DECEMBER 29

A fine, worn, handsome face, a face that was like an open letter in a foreign tongue.

DECEMBER 30

The little waxed *salle a manger* was sallow and sociable; Francois dancing over it, all smiles, was a man and a brother; the high-shouldered *patronne*, with her high-held, much-rubbed hands, seemed always assenting exuberantly to something unsaid; the Paris evening, in short, was, for Strether in the very taste of the soup, in the goodness, as he was innocently pleased to think it, of the wine, in the pleasant coarse texture of the napkin and the crunch of the thick-crusted bread.

DECEMBER 31

BROWNING IN WESTMINSTER ABBEY, 1890

Just as his great sign to those who knew him was that he was a force of health, of temperament, of tone, so what he takes into the Abbey is an immense expression of life—of life rendered with large liberty and free experiment, with an unprejudiced intellectual eagerness to put himself in other people's place, to participate in complications and consequences—a restlessness of psychological research that might well alarm any pale company for their formal orthodoxies.

[ROBERT BROWNING BURIED IN WESTMINSTER ABBEY ON THIS DAY IN 1890]

Index of Sources